CHRISTIAN ETHICS

"Gilbert Meilaender's characteristic clarity and grace make *Christian Ethics* a delightfully refreshing read. Meilaender's elegance and sobriety manages what few writers about ethics can: he makes the spirit and structure of the Christian life sound like good news. This is a wonderful volume that every Christian would do well to read."

—**Matthew Lee Anderson**, assistant research professor of ethics and theology, Baylor University

"There is nobody—believer or unbeliever—who doesn't have important things to learn from the thought of Gilbert Meilaender. Although he writes as a Christian ethicist, anchored in the Lutheran tradition, he is a teacher of humanity. There is nothing narrowly 'sectarian' about his reflections and writings. The evidence for that is on display in each of the essays in this valuable collection. My advice to people of every faith (and none) is to read and learn."

—**Robert P. George**, McCormick Professor of Jurisprudence, Princeton University

"Gilbert Meilaender is for me one of the fathers in the recovery of the field of truly Christian ethics. This book conveys his mastery of theological ethics in the tradition and of philosophical ethics from Aristotle to contemporary thinkers. Most importantly this lucid introduction to ethics ensconces ethics within the gospel, within life in the triune God, within discipleship in Christ by the Spirit, and within an understanding of human personhood in community—thus surpassing, though not ignoring, consequentialist, deontological, and virtue approaches. From this vantage point he equips us to engage with all the challenging ethical issues of our time."

—**W. Ross Hastings**, Sangwoo Youtong Chee Chair of Theology, Regent College, Vancouver, British Columbia

"In this volume Meilaender encapsulates key themes traversing his work for years. Drawing together paradox and faith in theology and human experience, Meilaender approaches a broad range of significant topics shaping Christian ethics that markedly unifies love and obedience as central to life in Christ. A vital read for those trying to understand Protestant ethics more deeply through the rich foundational and practical questions of a life transformed through faith, hope, and love."

—**Autumn Alcott Ridenour**, Mockler Associate Professor of Christian Ethics, Gordon-Conwell Theological Seminary

"Meilaender serves us all by reminding us that Christian ethics is not self-improvement and virtue signaling. He discusses ethics vertically in light of the pardon and power of God's grace, manifesting horizontally in love toward one's neighbor. Individuals and congregations should study this insightful resource. I will be using it as an introductory college textbook."

—**Scott Stiegemeyer**, associate professor of theology and bioethics, Concordia University Irvine

ESSENTIALS *in Christian Ethics*

CHRISTIAN ETHICS

A Short Companion

Gilbert Meilaender

editors
C. Ben Mitchell & Jason Thacker

Christian Ethics: A Short Companion

Published by B&H Academic
Brentwood, Tennessee

ISBN: 978-1-4300-8748-9

Dewey Decimal Classification: 241
Subject Heading: CHRISTIAN LIFE \ RELIGIOUS \ CHRISTIAN ETHICS

The web addresses referenced in this book were live and correct at the time of the book's publication but may be subject to change.

Cover design by Emily Keafer Lambright.
Cover illustration by J614/iStock.

Printed in the United States of America

29 28 27 26 25 24 VP 1 2 3 4 5 6 7 8 9 10

In memory of my parents, with gratitude

CONTENTS

SERIES PREFACE

In 1876, German Lutheran theologian Christoph Ernst Luthardt eloquently illustrated the relationship between theology and ethics. He wrote, "God first loved us is the summary of Christian doctrine. We love Him is the summary of Christian morality."[1] The wedding of theology and ethics was later embraced by generations of theologians and ethicists, such as Protestant titans Herman Bavinck and Carl F. H. Henry,[2] who rightly understood the primacy of both theology and ethics in the Christian life. But at times in the recent history of the Protestant church, the study of ethics has been relegated to a mere application of theology and biblical studies rather than understood as a first-order discipline in rich partnership with the theological task.

The aim of the Christian ethic can be summed up in the words of Jesus in Matt 22:37–39. We, God's people, are to "love the Lord

[1] Christoph Ernst Luthardt, *Apologetic Lectures on the Moral Truths of Christianity*, trans. Sophia Taylor (Edinburgh: T&T Clark, 1876), 26.

[2] See Herman Bavinck, *Reformed Ethics*. ed. John Bolt, vol. 1, *Created, Fallen, and Converted Humanity* (Grand Rapids: Baker, 2019), §1:58; and Carl F. H. Henry, *Christian Personal Ethics*, 2nd ed. (Grand Rapids: Baker, 1979), 486.

[our] God with all [our] heart[s] and with all [our] soul[s] and with all [our] mind[s] . . . and to love [our] neighbor as [ourselves]." We hear echoes of this summation in the words of Luthardt, Bavinck, and Henry, each of whom spoke of how God's people are to love him as the summary of Christian morality. Thus, Christian ethics is nothing less than a primary motivation for those seeking to be faithful to God in all of life and live in light of how he has revealed himself in Scripture. Ethics as discipleship is a key theme throughout Scripture and one the church must elevate as we seek God's face in the academy, in our churches, and especially in our personal lives as transformed creatures made in the very image of God.

While Christian ethics is a core element of God's revelation to his people about how they are to live as his followers, it is also a distinct philosophical discipline that must be studied in consideration of the rich history of moral thought seen throughout the life of the church and the wider society. Much of today's discourse about Christian ethics tends to focus on the mere application of theological or philosophical principles, rather than understanding how these principles have been derived and refined over time in light of the massive metaphysical and epistemological shifts in the history of thought.

Given the recent tendency in wider evangelicalism at times to downplay the direct study of ethics in our curricula, in our church life, and in the task of discipleship, the Essentials in Christian Ethics series is designed to illuminate the richness of the Christian ethic, as well as how ethics is intricately woven into the whole of the Christian life. We have gathered renowned ethicists and leading figures in their fields of theological and philosophical inquiry who are passionate about proclaiming the biblical ethic to a world desperately in need of Christ.

The series is made up of short, introductory volumes spanning metaethics, normative ethics, and applied ethics. Each volume can be used independently as an introduction to the crucial elements of the Christian ethical tradition, including resources for further reading and key concepts for those seeking to dig deeper into the beauty of God's revelation. They can also be used as supplements to a larger ethics curriculum, where a specialized volume could be used to augment a primary text or to give deeper insight into particular contemporary ethical debates.

As editors, we have longed for a series like this to be written by scholars who understand and apply the rich relationship of theology and ethics in their teaching, writings, and ministry. This series is designed to model for readers how the biblical ethic applies to every area of life both as a distinct theological and philosophical discipline in the context of the Christian moral tradition from a robust Protestant viewpoint. We pray this serves the wider academy, those training in our colleges and seminaries, and especially those seeking to employ the riches of Christian ethics in the context of the local church.

C. Ben Mitchell and Jason Thacker
Series Editors

INTRODUCTION

There are surely many ways one might construct a "short companion" to Christian ethics, and there is no single right way to do it. In these few introductory paragraphs, I aim simply to outline the approach I will be taking.

When Christians think about how they are to live, they necessarily think of their lives always in relation to God. And that means the God whom we have come to know in Jesus—the God who orders human life in creation; the God from whom we have turned and to whom we need to find our way back; and the God who, never giving up on us, comes in search of us when we cannot find the way back. That simple threefold relation to God provides the central movements in the narrative that gives structure to the Christian life and shapes the spirit within which it is lived.

If we think of human beings as God's creatures, we cannot suppose that we could or should determine entirely for ourselves the plan for our lives. Much as we love the freedom to choose for ourselves, and important as it often is to exercise such freedom, we are, after all, dependent beings. The Author of our being has authority over us. We never belong to anyone else, or to any human community, to the whole extent of our being. Hence, when we think about how we ought to live, we try to take seriously the ways in which the Creator has ordered human life, and we realize that freedom is not the sole truth about our nature. For that reason one of the things this book attempts is to think about how to structure our lives so that we follow what the psalmist calls the way of the righteous and are like trees planted by streams of water, whose leaf does not wither.

As the psalmist also knew, we often fail to be such people. The way of the righteous is not the only possibility; there is also the way of the wicked. And, however hard it may be for us sometimes to acknowledge this, it is precisely the independence we love that underlies our wrong turnings. Flying in the face of reality, we try to live as if our lives were entirely our own. To think about the Christian life, therefore, is also to think about how sin permeates and distorts our lives. Herbert Butterfield, who was a well-known British historian, once wrote that if we were to take the animosity present in the average church choir and give it a dimension over time by giving it a history, we would have an explanation for all the wars that have been fought in human history. Hence, to think about the Christian life is to think not only of ways in which the Creator has ordered our lives but also about our own tendency to disorder them.

This short companion invites us, therefore, to think about the structure of the Christian life—what we are to do and who we are to be; our sin and the grace of God that brings pardon and healing to sinful people; the meaning of a life that responds to the call of God and is lived within the church. When we think about the structure of the Christian life, these topics are almost unavoidable, and we consider them in Part One of the book.

Important as those topics are, none of them captures fully what we might call the inner spirit of Christian living, a spirit of love that marks God's continued search for his wandering creatures—a search that culminates in Jesus' mission and ministry, his death and resurrection. And, as St. Paul writes in Romans 5, this spirit of love has been poured into our hearts through Jesus' own Spirit. Whatever else we may say about the Christian life, therefore, we must think about the meaning of that love. Directed toward God and our neighbors, it may not always be easy or pleasant. No doubt God intends our happiness, but the way to that end is seldom straightforward. For that reason the second half of this book explores in some detail the meaning (and the complications) of Christian love.

Taken together, these two parts—structure and spirit—seek to unfold at least some of the central elements in the Christian way of life. Rather than supposing that we could creatively fashion our own moral vision, the aim here is to think within an inherited Christian tradition of thought. Something similar is true in many other areas of life. The historian Robert Wilken once suggested that we try listening to writers and players of jazz or folk music. When they speak of their teachers and masters, it is with respect. They note how they first learned to play by imitating someone else's style. So their own creativity, and their way to excellence, comes from working within the tradition and exploring its intricacies. It is, therefore, with similar respect that we try here to chart a way to live with an obedience shaped by love as we seek to explore a few central themes central to the structure and spirit of the Christian life.

We could, I suppose, describe this as a book about Christian ethics, but perhaps that would not be the most apt description. Christian ethics is, after all, an academic discipline. Its practitioners converse primarily with each other as they try to sort out and clarify a range of complicated issues. Their work is significant, and we would not want to be without it. But here I aim at something just a little different: reflection on the shape of the Christian life.

No doubt there is much more that could be said about that than I say here, and no doubt this book will not do justice to the richness and intricacy of the Christian life, but perhaps it at least makes a useful beginning. And in the living of the Christian life, the most important thing is surely to begin.

PART I

The Structure of the Christian Life

ONE

Three Models of Moral Reasoning

In *Mere Christianity*, using the sort of illustration that seemed to come effortlessly to him, C. S. Lewis pointed to three considerations that are important for the moral life.

> Think of us first as a fleet of ships sailing in formation. The voyage will be a success only, in the first place, if the ships do not collide and get in one another's way; and, secondly, if each ship is seaworthy and has her engines in good order. As a matter of fact, you cannot have either of these two things without the other. If the ships keep on having collisions they will not remain seaworthy very long. On the other hand, if their steering gears are out of order they will not be able to avoid collisions. . . . But there is one thing we have not yet taken into account. We have not asked where the fleet is trying to get to. . . . And however

> well the fleet sailed, its voyage would be a failure if it were meant to reach New York and actually arrived at Calcutta.[1]

The analogy calls our attention to three important elements in moral reasoning. We might refer to them as duties, virtues, and results. Or we could talk of what makes action right (avoiding collisions), what makes character praiseworthy (the engines must be in good order), and what good(s) we should aim at in our action (the desired destination).

Morality—and thinking about the moral life—necessarily involves all three of these. We think about right and wrong, duty and obligation. We consider the virtues and vices that may mark our character. And we think about our goals, the results we are trying to produce in our action.

Although serious moral reflection will always involve all three angles of vision, each of us is likely to make one of them central in our thinking, even as we try not to ignore the importance of the other two. Because any of the three can be made our central concern, we may distinguish three different models for doing ethics: a "consequentialist" ethic whose unifying motif is a focus on our goals and the results of our action; a "deontological" ethic whose unifying motif focuses on the language of duties and rights; and an "agent-centered" ethic of character, which, unlike the other two angles, focuses less on our doing than our being. As we think through and compare these three ways of ordering our moral thinking, we can also consider what place they should have more specifically in Christian moral reflection.

A consequentialist ethic

In *The Responsible Self* H. Richard Niebuhr noted three different ways we might think of human beings. One of these is to picture ourselves as makers or fashioners—as craftsmen seeking to produce something worthwhile or valuable. We are in the world as people who have projects. Thinking of human beings in this way, we naturally focus especially on possible results of our action, and, Niebuhr suggested, the question we ask ourselves is "What is valuable? What results are good?"

Of course, in almost every case, our possible courses of action are likely to produce different results—some good, others not so good. Our task then, at least as this sort of moral craftsman believes, is to find the course of action that seems likely to produce the greatest value overall—the action that will produce the best consequences. This way of thinking about the moral life, with its emphasis on producing the greatest net-benefit for all affected by our action, has had considerable appeal—in utilitarian approaches to ethics, for example.

Another way to describe this approach is to say that for consequentialist moral thinking an "ought to do" follows from an "ought to be." Thus, if it ought to be the case that no one suffer horribly while dying, we ought to do whatever is necessary to relieve or minimize such suffering. Sometimes, perhaps, it may even be that we ought to do what might ordinarily seem wrong—as, for example, deliberately kill in order to relieve terrible suffering. We might hesitate to endorse this sort of moral reasoning, of course, worrying that we are allowing a good end to justify a questionable means to that end. No doubt such hesitation is warranted, but once we give good results priority in our moral thinking, it may seem that a sufficiently good end can justify a means that might otherwise seem wrong. What else could, once we think of ourselves primarily as craftsmen, aiming to fashion the best product possible? If good results count most of all in morality, there can, in the end, be no other, independent, limit on the means we adopt to reach our goals.

One of the reasons consequentialist reasoning appeals to us is that it seems to make ethical thinking more like a science. We are invited to think of a scale on which we weigh the various possible outcomes, calculating which action will be best on the whole. In addition, we may be drawn to this approach because it has a kind of "progressive" feel, focusing, as it does, on future well-being. This model of moral reasoning quite naturally appeals to those who are pragmatic and goal-oriented, those eager to demystify moral problems and find technical solutions for them.

For different reasons it may also sometimes appeal to Christians. After all, Christian understandings of the moral life have often emphasized words like *love* and *freedom*. And, at least if we don't analyze it too carefully, "being loving" can sound a little like maximizing the well-being of as many people as possible. Love, as Christians sometimes depict it, may seem to require active concern for others, the sort of concern that wouldn't let a rule stand in the way of producing valuable results in others' lives. An emphasis on the language of freedom may press in the same direction. "The sabbath was made for man," Jesus says, "not man for the sabbath." If a saying such as that is the beginning and the end of our moral outlook, we may suppose that sometimes the good for others cannot be maximized unless we live in ways that are free from the restrictions of binding rules. Therefore, a consequentialist is likely to say, we must always be prepared to reexamine and revise our moral rules in the light of new insight into what will produce outcomes most valuable to others.

While this model of moral reasoning may seem attractive, it is not free of problems and difficulties. Perhaps the most fundamental of these lies at the very heart of the model. A consequentialist ethic asks us to try to look at life from the perspective of what the philosopher Henry Sidgwick called "the eye of the universe." This is a view from nowhere in particular and, hence, it may not really suit human beings who are embodied and located, who occupy a particular place that carries its own special responsibilities. To think of ourselves as the sort of agents consequentialists recommend is to exaggerate our responsibility for the state of the world—to think of ourselves as godlike. It exhibits what the political theorist Michael Sandel—writing in particular about genetic enhancement—called a "drive to mastery."[2] Once we begin to think in this way, imagining we can construct a science of moral reasoning, we may easily exaggerate our ability to predict and control the outcomes of our actions, and we may mistakenly suppose that we can really find a way to reduce the great diversity of possible, valuable outcomes to some single common denominator such as love. While it is true that we are craftsmen, that we are in the world as people who have projects, there is more than just this to say about human beings. We may, then, want to consider a second model of moral reasoning.

A deontological ethic

A second characterization of human beings suggested by H. Richard Niebuhr was that of the fellow-citizen. Rather than thinking of ourselves primarily as crafting a product or fashioning an outcome, we could think of ourselves more in political terms—as citizens living together in community under shared laws. After all, there is more to say about us than that we are people who have goals. It is just as important to note that we pursue those outcomes while living in community with others who have a dignity like our own, a dignity that should be respected.

Hence, we must ask ourselves not only what outcomes would be good but also what is right—that is, what law should govern our interactions with others. Starting with this question, we will need to consider not only the goods we would like to produce, but also our actions themselves—whether they are right or wrong. From this perspective, what we *do* is more central to the moral life than what we *accomplish*. This kind of moral theory is often called "deontological," from the Greek word *deon*, which refers to what is binding.

Because right actions rather than good outcomes are central in this model, even a good end will not necessarily justify any and every means to that end. There may be some actions that ought not be done, even if they would achieve results that are, on the whole, desirable. For consequentialists, the moral world has a kind of unity; the right act simply is the act that will produce the greatest good. But for deontologists the right and the good are distinct moral judgments that may not always be reconcilable, if there is no right way to achieve the desired outcome. Of course, deontologists will believe that we have a duty to bring aid where we can and to seek good results. But we are also obligated to refrain from doing wrong, and the requirements of justice set independent limits on our attempts to produce good outcomes. We should do as much good as we can, but that means as much good as we *morally* can.

Therefore, to adhere to this second model of moral reasoning is to agree with St. Paul that we ought not do evil that good may come of it. Our responsibility to seek good outcomes is always shaped and governed by the obligation not to do what is wrong (even when it might seem to lead to desirable results). Both Jews and Christians have traditionally acknowledged that the "right" is in this way prior to the "good." So, for instance, the Talmud forbade handing over a hostage to be killed, even if refusing to do so would lead to a similar fate for a greater number of people. And more generally, the concept of "covenant" that is so central in both Jewish and Christian belief teaches us to think of ourselves as agents bound by claims of fiduciary loyalty that should be honored and upheld. To have covenanted with others is to have obligations that should not be broken even in order to achieve good results. We are not just agents who seek to produce the greatest good possible; we are trustees for others, bound by particular claims of covenant loyalty to them.

To see this is to see the crucial difference between consequentialist and deontological models—and it is, in the end, a theological difference. For this second model our responsibility to produce good results, while genuine and important, is always limited by the obligation to avoid wrongdoing. If the moral world—the good and the right—sometimes seem to fall apart, we are not agents whose drive to mastery must seek to unify them by doing evil in the service of good. To be sure, this may sometimes leave us with unanswered questions, when our duties seem to clash. Nonetheless, we do not see with the eye of the universe, and to restore unity of the good and the right in a broken world is, in the end, God's task, not ours.

The distinction between these two models of moral reasoning gets at something that is central in human life. We can see that if we set moral argument aside for the moment and consider an example from baseball. The philosopher Alva Noë, in his book *Infinite Baseball: Notes from a Philosopher at the Ballpark* (Oxford, 2019) pointed to a difference between two pitching feats that are in some respects closely related—a perfect game and a no-hitter. A pitcher can throw a no-hitter even while losing the game; indeed, that has happened. The outcome of the game is not what determines whether a no-hitter has been thrown. The quality of being a no-hitter "floats free of outcomes," as Noë says. And life can be like that. It is not the outcome but the intention that determines the nature of the act and "marks the differences between murder, justifiable homicide, and accidental killing."

Not so with a perfect game. Because the opposing team gets no runners on base, a pitcher cannot lose a perfect game. It is the outcome—and only it—that determines whether a perfect game has been thrown, and sometimes that may be what we attend to. After all, whether because of murder, justifiable homicide, or accidental killing, it is still true that a human being has been killed. The outcome is the same, which is why we grieve. But the nature of the act may not be the same, since the agent's intention in acting will help us decide whether to label it an act of murder, justifiable homicide, or accidental killing—and to apportion moral responsibility and blame accordingly.

In short, these two models of moral reasoning treat as central quite different aspects of human action. And, in the end, the choice between them turns on whether we think human beings are responsible for all the outcomes their actions produce—whether our responsibility is that extensive and godlike, or whether as embodied and located creatures we must in the end leave outcomes to God.

An ethic of character

However different the first two models may be, they are alike in one way: each focuses on a judgment about actions, about what we ought to do. The third model is different; it focuses less on our *doing* than on our *being*. It emphasizes neither the good nor the right, but character, our virtues and vices. From this angle of vision we think of human beings less as makers or citizens than as—to use Niebuhr's terms—responders or answerers. We are constantly responding to and being shaped by events around us, and our actions both shape and express our character.

Rather than thinking of ourselves simply as those who pursue goals or adhere to rules of right, we might consider how we are constantly responding to what goes on around us—which means, in the end, responding to the actions of God in our world. Consider, Niebuhr suggested, what it is like for the driver of an automobile, who must make countless decisions at every moment. It will not suffice for him simply to obey the rules of the road set down in the driver's manual; for sometimes doing so may cause harm. Nor can he simply drive in the direction of his desired destination, regardless of what he sees in front of him on the road.

Thus, morally discerning action depends on becoming the sort of person who can respond appropriately in a variety of circumstances. To use an older language, our character needs to be shaped by virtues that help us see what needs to be done. If the consequentialist model invites us to think of ethics almost as a science, this agent-centered model turns in a very different direction. Our character affects what we *see* when we look around, and sound moral judgment depends on accumulated experience, developed sensitivities, wise exemplars, a good community—and divine guidance.

This third model of moral reasoning has always played a significant role in Christian thought. Attention to the nature of virtue and vice has a long history in Roman Catholic moral theology (where the influence of Aristotle's ethic of character has been important). At least until recently, when the language of virtue was reemphasized, Protestants have tended to use the language of motive, of holiness, or of "inner spirit," to draw attention to the importance of character. One of the strengths of this third model is that—in ways that go well beyond either of the first two models—it makes place for the role of religious communities and for disciplines such as prayer, confession, service, and praise. Such disciplines shape the self, they expand our moral vision, and they constantly reorient us in relation to God. Moral life becomes, to use common Christian language, a life lived "in the Spirit."

Despite these attractive features of an ethic of character, taken alone it is unlikely to be sufficient. It is better thought of as supplementing one of the first two models of moral reasoning. By itself it may well lead to a kind of moral relativism. After all, our character is formed not just in one overarching community but at least as much in many smaller sub-communities. Different people may have been shaped in quite different ways and may, therefore, respond to what goes on around them in equally different ways. This explains why an ethic of character may have difficulty dealing with public questions or helping us to find common ground in public life.

An even deeper problem may be embedded in an agent-centered ethic. The problem is precisely that: it is agent-centered! Alasdair MacIntyre once suggested that no account of morality could possibly be adequate if it did not reckon with the truth that adhering to what is right may require one's death at any moment.[3] My flourishing cannot be at the heart of morality. When in the late twentieth century there came to be renewed attention to an ethic of virtue, it was often characterized as focused on human flourishing (a way of thinking that has its roots in Aristotle). The idea is a simple one. Cultivating the virtues enables us to shape ourselves, to become more fully what human beings are meant to be—and in that sense to flourish. Nevertheless, while it is true that if we are virtuous we will in countless ways attend to the good of others, there remains something inevitably self-referential and self-serving about making cultivation of my character, rather than commitment to what I owe to others, central to the moral life.

The command and calling of God

Models of moral reasoning can do only so much, however, at least for Christians. To see what is required of us in any given circumstance is to discern something universal: what might be required of anyone similarly situated. But what is formal and universal, in a sense abstract, does not yet capture what is personal: our relation to the God who commands. What is asked of us does not change when we hear it as the command of God, but we receive it now as gift—not simply as command but also as calling. Even if we gain insight through moral reasoning, that insight does not become simply a possession we could hand on to others; for a personal relation, a calling, cannot be transmitted that way. Each must find it for himself or herself.

To see what the created order requires of us, to listen for the commands of God's law, becomes something more than an exercise in moral reasoning. It is now for us the life of discipleship, our attempt to follow Jesus in his obedience to his Father. And the life of discipleship is not an intellectual possession that can be handed on from one generation to the next. It is a journey that begins in faith and must regularly return to that starting point; it will not be achieved by clear, persuasive reasoning alone. We might keep in mind the witty comment of Johannes de Silentio in Kierkegaard's *Fear and Trembling*: "When learning how to make swimming movements, one can hang in a belt from the ceiling; one may be said to describe the movements all right but one isn't swimming." Likewise, our calling is not just to reason well, but, responding to the grace and mercy of God, to learn to swim.

TWO

Human Nature and Sin

It is one thing to say that we should respond to the grace and mercy of God by desiring to become people whose character is marked by virtue, who seek the good, and who aim to do what is right. But it is quite another actually to accomplish this in all that we do and say. To mark our failings here, Christians use the term *sin*, and to think about the nature of sin we should first say something about human nature. For sin must be in some sense a defection from our created nature.

We might characterize human beings as two-sided creatures, marked by a kind of duality. As Reinhold Niebuhr (influenced by Kierkegaard and, still farther back, St. Augustine) often put it, we stand at the juncture of nature and spirit, our lives characterized by both necessity and freedom. Put more simply, we are both finite and free.

A simple illustration has often helped me to illustrate this duality. Drop me from the top of a fifty-story building, and the law of gravity takes over just as surely as it would if a rock had been dropped. Finite human beings located in space and time are subject to natural necessities every bit as much as are objects such as rocks. But a human being dropped from that building is not simply a falling object, subject to the law of gravity. For as I fall, there are truths about my experience that could not be captured in the language of mass and velocity. For this falling human being is not only subject to nature's laws but is also characterized by self-awareness. I know myself as one who is falling, and in that sense freely transcend my finite location. To say that I can know myself as a falling object means that I can to some extent "distance" myself from that object. Somehow, and simultaneously, I both am and am not that object. More generally, we could say that human beings are able to experience themselves thinking—to be both the subject doing the thinking and the object being thought about, while yet experiencing oneself as a single whole.

Which is the real me? The finite body subject to biological and historical necessities? Or the free spirit that soars beyond those limits? The thought or the thinker? When we say that human beings are both, Christians are affirming that the real me is a single entity in whom there is duality, in whom the self mysteriously stands outside itself. To be sure, our created nature, even with its finite limitations, is a good that partially fulfills us, but there is something more than that to be said. Created for communion with God, the human heart is—as Augustine memorably put it at the outset of his *Confessions*—restless until it rests in God, until our free spirit has found a limit it cannot transcend.

Indeed, to ask which is the real me is the wrong question; the real me simply *is* the being who is this duality. We should not deny genuine significance to our natural, historical life. But neither should we try to find in it the full meaning of our humanity. When we fail to accept and appreciate the duality of our nature, we make of earthly life either everything (as if the heart were not still restless) or nothing (as if it were not God's good creation)—either ultimate or unimportant. But neither is true; the human person simply is the duality of nature and spirit. This gives rise, however, to an enormous instability in life. We can go wrong in two quite different ways, the sins of pride and sloth.

The sin of pride as Christians understand it is something quite different from a little harmless vanity. On the contrary, it lies at the root of other sins and distorts all our loves. As finite creatures we are dependent beings, unable to live solely within ourselves, out of our own resources. Hence, our happiness and security depend on something outside ourselves. That can be a bitter pill to swallow for people like us, who want to be independent and to control our own destiny. There is a nice illustration of this in *Perelandra*, one of C. S. Lewis's space fantasies. Perelandra is a newly created and unfallen world made up mostly of floating islands, although it does also have a Fixed Land. The central figure in this world, referred to simply as the Lady, is bound by the commands of Maleldil, the creator of Perelandra. In particular, she and the King (who seldom appears in the story) are not to live or sleep on the Fixed Land. They may go onto it but are not to stay there.

Just that becomes the source of her temptation. The Unman, through whom evil powers seek to infiltrate Perelandra and destroy its created goodness, uses this simple prohibition—not to sleep on the Fixed Land—to unsettle the Lady and create uncertainty in her. When she misses the King, who is elsewhere, the Unman notes that people who live on a Fixed Land cannot so easily be separated. They are not constantly "thrown into the wave" and can to some extent control their own destinies. He tells the Lady that the command to live only on the floating islands comes "between you and all settled life, all command of your days." And this is, of course, true. Eventually, though, when the Unman's temptations have been overcome, the Lady sees the point of the prohibition.

> The reason for not yet living on the Fixed Land is now so plain. How could I wish to live there except because it was Fixed? And why should I desire the Fixed except to make sure—to be able one day to command where I should be the next and what should happen to me. It was to reject the wave—to draw my hands out of Maleldil's, to say to Him, "Not thus, but thus"—to put in our own power what times should roll toward us . . . as if you gathered fruits together to-day for tomorrow's eating instead of taking what came. That would have been cold love and feeble trust.[4]

To be finite is to be thrown constantly into the wave, never to be entirely in control. Had we trust enough, we could no doubt live that way, but we prefer to govern and direct our own lives.

Pride is simply this attempt to secure ourselves, to exercise freedom without limit. It is, as William F. May put it in *A Catalogue of Sins*, "the sin of the first person singular." Hence, in its very nature pride is antisocial, since the desire to be godlike can allow for no competitors. This does not mean that the fruits of pride are always or obviously evil. The most law-abiding and seemingly virtuous people among us may—like the man in Jesus' parable who gave tithes of all that he possessed—do much that is good in the world.

Nonetheless, in pride we try to pretend that we are all freedom—that we can live independently out of our own resources, entrusting our life to no one, not even to God. Describing Satan's sin in his *City of God* (11.13) St. Augustine gives the classical description of pride: "He refused to be subject to his creator, and in his arrogance supposed that he wielded power as his own private possession." And Augustine goes on at once to add: "He has refused to accept reality." For in pride we make war on the truth of the universe, struggling to live as if we were not dependent beings. And however appealing this may sometimes seem, it cannot work, and we must ultimately fail to flourish.

Sloth

Just as pride is not vanity, sloth is not laziness. Like pride, it arises as a reaction to our insecurity. One sort of anxiety is created by our finitude and dependence—the anxiety that comes from being dependent on another for our wellbeing. But freedom can also be terrifying. To be called beyond the limits to which we are accustomed—old attachments, communities, and loves—can create a kind of frightening vertigo. In reaction we might flee from our freedom back to the comfortable world to which we are accustomed. Whereas pride may move us to suppose we are free simply to remake the natural world, sloth moves us to fall back into the world of limited commitments and the given world in which we feel at home. This can never really satisfy, for the call beyond comfortable limits is, in the end, a call to rest the heart in God. Clinging in sloth to whatever makes us feel at ease, we are afraid to respond to that call from the One for whom we are made, and we are unlikely to delight for long in the good gifts of creation.

The truth is that all genuine pleasures of life come from the hand of God. They are shafts of the Creator's glory, penetrating our world not only to give us joy but also to point us to God. That, however, is just what the slothful man or woman fears. We fear acknowledging our need for something more than the given pleasures of life. And so, we choke off the longing that draws us out of ourselves to God, supposing that created goods can bear the whole weight of the heart's longing. But that is to ask of them more than they can give, for they are meant to lead beyond themselves. That is why sloth is not simply laziness. It is more like apathy or boredom. Beginning with an inability really to desire God, it ends in boredom more generally—an inability to delight even in the good gifts of creation. After all, they cannot finally satisfy the longing of our hearts; they were never meant to.

In our pride and sloth we inevitably produce idols. It is clear enough how sloth might move us to create idols. For in sloth we cling desperately to good persons or things, as if they might satisfy our deepest longings. But pride can also lead to the creation of idols, even if not in so obvious a way. In his *City of God* St. Augustine gives an example of this in his discussion of the temptation of Adam and Eve. He writes that, although Eve was deceived by the serpent, Adam was not. Why then did he also sin? Because he was so "closely bound" to her that he "refused to be separated from his only companion, even if it involved sharing her sin." There is a kind of nobility and grandeur to such devotion, but it is founded in a pride that does not want to accept God's ordering of the world. And so he must make of his partner more than she really is, an idol.

The destination of all sin, both the sins rooted in pride and those that grow from sloth, is, as William F. May noted, solitude. "The solitary self to which pride is devoted in its final stages is at one and the same time the bored self." In that solitary end we see what has been true of sin from its beginning—a slothful inability or a prideful unwillingness to love. In the end it leaves us, as C. S. Lewis wrote (in his Preface to *The Screwtape Letters*), with "the ruthless, sleepless, unsmiling concentration upon self which is the mark of Hell." No wonder Christians look not to their own accomplishments but to the grace of God for deliverance from this self-imposed prison.

Sin as a Condition

The problem of sin from which we need deliverance goes even deeper into our character than the sins of pride and sloth, deeper than even the best moral reasoning or ethical theory can fix. Nothing within our power to do or accomplish, no virtuous trait that we might develop, can solve this problem, for it is a condition in which we find ourselves from the start. That condition Christians have sometimes called original sin.

We may be tempted to suppose that Christian teaching about original sin provides an explanation for the presence of sin in a creation pronounced "good" by its Creator. The truth, however, is that it does not really offer such an explanation, nor is that its point. We can see this if we consider what has probably been the most important biblical passage for thinking about original sin, some verses from Romans chapter 5. Referring to the story of Adam, St. Paul writes, "Sin came into the world through one man and death through sin, and so death spread to all men because all men sinned." That sin notwithstanding, the free gift of righteousness and new life has come through another man, Jesus. Thus, "as by one man's disobedience many were made sinners, so by one man's obedience many will be made righteous." Indeed, "where sin increased, grace abounded all the more."

Hence the reason for St. Paul's appeal to the sin of Adam seems less to explain the pervasiveness and unavoidability of sin than to point to the story of Jesus, to underscore how great a deliverance God has worked through him. It turns out that in order to tell the story of Jesus correctly, we cannot avoid also confessing the depth of human slavery to sin. No training in virtue, no help from moral exemplars, not even the best of ethical theories can break the chains of that slavery. Not even Jesus as moral exemplar. So, for example, in his *Confessions* St. Augustine observes how in his journey to faith there was a time when he "thought of Christ my Lord only as a man of excellent wisdom which none could equal." But that was not enough to overcome the condition of "harsh bondage" from which—because, with his loves divided he was in conflict with himself—he could not break free.

St. Paul characterizes our condition in this way not in order to talk about sin or demean the goodness of our created nature, but to announce and marvel at the fact that "where sin increased, grace abounded all the more." If, therefore, we believe and live within the story of Jesus, we will not seek to minimize the power of sin; for only he could break that power. Only when we see God's solution to our sin do we realize just how deep within us the problem lies. Hence, belief in sin as a condition in which we simply find ourselves does not begin with a theory about sin; it begins with Jesus and the gift of new life that came in him. The aim is not to unfold some strange and baffling teaching of which no sense can be made, nor is it intended to focus on particular misdeeds. Instead, it focuses on a *condition* in which we simply find ourselves—a condition in which, as we come from the womb, we are both unable and unwilling to avoid sinning.

Once we see this, we should also realize what the story in Genesis of humanity's Fall into sin does *not* do. It does not explain how sin could have entered a perfect world; rather, it leaves sin unexplained—a surd in the universe. Indeed, before our first parents ever sin in that Genesis story, sin is already inexplicably present in the tempter. All we can say is that, despite the insecurity produced by the duality of our nature, it was not inevitable that human beings should sin. One way to make the point is to say, as C. S. Lewis does in *The Problem of Pain*, that if other rational species exist somewhere in the universe, "it is not necessary to suppose that they also have fallen."

None of this is to deny that the concept of original sin is and always will be puzzling. After all, the noun "sin" suggests an action for which we bear responsibility, even while the adjective "original" seems to imply that things could not have been otherwise, that sin has been our condition from the start and that there was never a moment when we stood on neutral ground, able to sin or not to sin. Still, puzzling as it may be, we need not simply throw up our hands and give up any attempt at understanding. C. S. Lewis once suggested (in *The Problem of Pain*) that we imagine a story about a boy raised in terrible circumstances, his character marked by countless vices. He is, let us suppose, a liar, a petty thief, a bully. Now, however, he is brought to live in a decent and caring family. When he behaves badly the other family members rightly remind themselves that the condition in which he started life was not really his fault. Nevertheless, as Lewis put it, we "cannot quite call his character a 'misfortune' *as if he were one thing and his character another.*" Alas, this—this liar, thief, bully—is who he is. "And if he begins to mend he will inevitably feel shame and guilt at what he is just beginning to cease to be." He found himself in a condition that he did not create; yet, the more his character improves, the more he will realize that he must take responsibility for that condition. Indeed, although we like to think of ourselves as independent individuals, before we are even able to think of ourselves that way, our character had already been formed in countless respects.

There is no starting over from the beginning.

> Our humanity itself is a cultural heritage; the talking animal is talked into talk by those who talk at him; and how if they talk crooked? His mind is not at first his own, but the echo of his elders. The echo turns into a voice, the painted portrait steps down from the frame, and each of us becomes himself. Yet by the time we are aware of our independence, we are what others have made us. We can never unweave the web to the very bottom, and weave it up again.[5]

"Why then," we might ask (as Augustine does in the *Confessions*) "are you relying on yourself, only to find yourself unreliable?" We need to look elsewhere, as St. Paul reminds us in Romans 5: "If many died through one man's trespass, much more have the grace of God and the free gift in the grace of that one man Jesus Christ abounded for many."

THREE

Grace as Power and Pardon

Forgiveness, as a form of love which is beyond good and evil, is bound to be offensive to pure moralists."[6] Thus, in one compact sentence, Reinhold Niebuhr articulated the difficulty of making place in the moral life for divine grace—or, alternatively, making place for ethics within a theology that accents grace.

If in Jesus God pardons and accepts us even in our sin, if indeed we are clothed with the righteousness of Christ, it might seem as if there were no need for anything more—no necessity for growth in virtue or progress in the moral life. Whatever our behavior, it will still be true that God loves and accepts sinners. That is, after all, what St. Paul writes in Romans 5: "while we were yet sinners Christ died for us." Of course, this is the same Paul who writes in Philippians 2: "Work out your own salvation with fear and trembling; for God is at work in you, both to will and to work for his good pleasure." Clearly, there is something puzzling here that needs our attention.

God's grace meets us, it seems, as both pardon and power. To say everything that must be said of that grace, we will need to look at it from two quite different angles—and only then, having done so, can we consider how, if at all, these two approaches may be reconciled.

Grace as power

The first approach we may call "grace as power." From this perspective we emphasize that the Spirit of Christ empowers us to become people who more and more please God—and, indeed, want to please God. The grace of God in Christ meets us where we are—that is, it meets us as people who regularly sin in many different ways. Yet, God meets us where we are not only to assure us that, despite our sins, we are pardoned and forgiven, but also to help us become less marked by sinful habits and behaviors—to grow in his grace and become increasingly intent on living in ways that keep God's commands and serve the needs of others. Divine grace is, therefore, the power of Christ *in* us, and without that power no real progress in the Christian life is possible. We can even say, then, that the Christian moral life is grounded in grace alone—*sola gratia*.

If we describe the work of grace this way, as the power of Christ's Spirit in us, helping us to become people who more and more please God, how are we picturing the presence of sin in our lives? Not so much, it would seem, in the singular (sin), as a condition in which we find ourselves. But more in the plural (sin*s*)—that is, quantitatively. Not so much a condition of faithlessness that marks us, for which again and again we need to be pardoned. But more as particular failings that need to be forgiven and overcome as we make progress in Christian living. To be sure, those sins (in the plural) may express and have their root in our sinful condition, but from the perspective of grace as power we think of them more piecemeal—as mistaken turns that need to be corrected and overcome.

Moreover, it is difficult to imagine fellowship with God, life in God's presence, unless they have been overcome, unless and until we are no longer inclined to sin. We might say, therefore, that fellowship with God can only happen on the level of holiness—when we have been healed by the power of God's grace and made whole. Indeed, could we even imagine the saints in heaven as people whose loves are still divided and whose character is still drawn toward sins of different sorts? On the contrary, we must picture them as people who have been made whole by the healing power of God's grace, the power of the Spirit of Christ.

This healing takes time. And we might think of "grace as power" as God's gift of time to us. From this perspective we can depict the Christian life as a journey in which—always empowered by divine grace—a sinner becomes more and more a saint, someone whose character and behavior can please God. When, as the Gospel of Mark records (2:1ff.), a paralyzed man was brought by his friends to Jesus for healing, Jesus forgave him for his sins. But Jesus did more. "Get up and walk," he said. The grace Jesus showed the man was not only pardon for wrongdoings but also power for new life.

"Get up and walk," Jesus says, calling each of us to the journey of Christian life. Along the way, of course, our wills remain divided, drawn in part toward the holiness to which God calls us and in part still drawn to sin, not yet whole and entire—neither simply saint nor simply sinner. Nevertheless, we can say that this journey of the Christian life is going somewhere; the power of God's grace can enable growth and progress in holiness. Of course, we cannot always trace such progress as a steady and unbroken line, as if it could easily or obviously be quantified or charted. But the very image of "backsliding," which Christians have sometimes used, suggests a possibility for progress from which we may sometimes fall back. And if we do fall back, we need to repent and do the works we did before, as the Seer in Revelation (2:5) says to the church in Ephesus.

Thus, we cannot say all that we need to say about the Christian life unless we make place for the empowering grace of Christ's Spirit in us. To be sure, this way of thinking about grace is not without its dangers; for it may invite a problematic concentration upon oneself. Two of these dangers, which are opposite sides of the same coin, deserve to be noted here. The first danger is presumption. Precisely insofar as we sometimes make progress toward holiness in life's journey, we may lose sight of the truth that the whole of this journey is the work of God's grace in us. We may begin to suppose that we have a claim on God, a holiness that even God must acknowledge and approve. Like the man in Jesus' parable recounted in Luke's Gospel (18:9ff.), we may be all too eager to call attention to our fasting and tithing. And, indeed, that man, a Pharisee, was not simply deceived. In many respects he was surely a very good man, for the Pharisees were deeply pious and devoted to Israel's God. But presuming himself to be farther along than he actually was on the journey toward righteousness, he did not see how divided his character remained.

The second danger is despair. Thinking of grace as the power of Christ's Spirit within us, we are invited to look inward—to take our spiritual temperature, so to speak, and consider how far along the path toward holiness we have traveled. When we do that, the answer may not always be an encouraging one. If we do not seem to be getting anywhere, and if we know that by the power of God's grace the Christian life is going somewhere, progressing toward holiness, we may be tempted to conclude that grace has not been at work in us. We seem to be entirely on our own in the journey of life—reason enough sometimes to despair.

To find ourselves in that condition is to see that, important as it is to think of grace as the power of Christ's Spirit within us, a different picture of grace is sometimes essential.

Grace as pardon

This second approach we may call "grace as pardon." Lest, looking for evidence that Christ lives in us, we fall into either presumption or despair, this approach constantly reminds us that in Christ God is *for* us. And he is for us precisely as he finds us—that is to say, he is for us even in our sin. From this perspective the fellowship with God that we desire and need is no longer postponed for a future time, placed as the endpoint of a long journey toward righteousness. Instead, we know Jesus as he is so often pictured in the Gospels—as the friend of sinners, whom we are called to trust in life and in death. The Christian life becomes first and foremost an invitation to trust that, unlovable as we may often be, God nevertheless pardons our failings and stands by our side.

Although this second approach focuses not on power but on pardon, it can in its own way be powerful and energizing. Freed from the necessity of regularly checking our spiritual temperature or wondering whether we are making sufficient progress on the journey toward holiness, we can focus on the needs of all those others whom Jesus calls our neighbors. Trusting that, come what may, God is on our side means that the energy we might have poured into trying to secure ourselves is available now for the various forms of service God sets before us in our different callings.

If we think in these terms, of grace as pardon, how are we picturing the presence of sin in our lives? No longer quantitatively and in the plural (sin*s*). But in the singular, as a condition (sin) in which we find ourselves. Not so much as a list of failings that need to be overcome as we seek to progress more and more in the Christian life, but as the faithlessness into which we fall again and again, continually needing to be pardoned. In fact, it is our condition of sinfulness that accounts for the particular sins we regularly commit. Every particular sin seems to presuppose a prior condition of sin. We can never get behind it, behind the division within the self that marks us and that gives rise to particular wrongdoings. The problem always goes a little deeper than we suppose.

Thinking of grace as pardon, we have to picture sin less in substantive than in relational terms. That is, our problem is not simply particular sins that we commit; our problem is that we are not in right relation with God. And this is not a condition that admits of less and more, that can be thought of quantitatively. We either are or are not in right relation with God. In fact, we are both simultaneously. Looked at as we are in ourselves, marked by that condition of sin, we are not right with God. Therefore, we are wholly and entirely sinners. Looked at as we are in Christ, who is for us, we are wholly and entirely righteous. Our task in life is not so much to make progress in holiness as simply to believe that the real truth about ourselves is that we are accepted by God—right with God, because Christ is for us.

In pardoning and accepting us even in our sinful condition, God continually reestablishes us in right relation with himself. Just as regularly, of course, that condition of sin reasserts itself, disrupting our relation to God. And for this second understanding of grace—grace as pardon—that is pretty much the story of Christian life. Again and again sin draws us away from right relation with

God. Again and again the word that in Christ God is for us restores our peace with God. If the "grace as power" model teaches us to think of the Christian life as going somewhere—progressing by God's grace toward the holiness that makes fellowship with God possible—the "grace as pardon" model might be said to teach us that the Christian life is going nowhere. On the contrary, the Christian life is simply beginning over and over, again and again, returning time after time to the word of pardon, which assures us we are accepted by God even in our sinfulness. We never really progress beyond that starting point. Nor need we. We need only trust the pardoning word of God.

We noted earlier that the "grace as power" approach brings, along with its strengths, certain characteristic dangers. So too does the "grace as pardon" approach. The problem now is not so much an undue concentration upon self as it is, instead, a kind of loss of self, which may happen in either of two ways. First, in our understandable desire to underscore the continuing faithfulness of God and to avoid turning inward to focus on our own spiritual condition, we risk becoming almost indifferent to progress in the moral life. Such indifference does not take seriously the gift of time God gives us, a time in which the Spirit of Christ is at work in us. We are, after all, instructed, "look carefully then how you walk, . . . making the most of the time" (Eph. 5:15ff.).

A second way in which this loss of self can occur goes even deeper. Because the "grace as pardon" model emphasizes not progress in Christian living but, instead, the constant need to repent of ourselves and begin again by the grace of God, we may experience something like a constant shattering of our aims and desires—a negation of the self. And while this—or something like it—will at times characterize our life as Christians, we never stop being God's good creatures. There is at least one aspect of our creaturely condition that ought never be negated: namely, the desire, the thirst, for God. That thirst is a mark of the creature's fundamental neediness, of our neediness. To suppose that, in order to magnify the grace of God, we must shatter and relinquish even that desire for God would be to turn a loss of self once again into an assertion of self—as if we should set the terms for God's acceptance of us.

Grace as power and pardon: Can they be reconciled?

Anyone familiar with twentieth-century theological literature about the work of divine grace in human lives may recognize that this discussion of grace as power and pardon has been influenced in many ways by the Swedish theologian Anders Nygren's great work, *Agape and Eros*.[7] "Grace as power" has many affinities with what Nygren calls Augustine's "caritas synthesis." And "grace as pardon" is not unlike Nygren's depiction of the renewal of the agape motif in Luther's theology. Nygren sees the two approaches as essentially incompatible, asserting that we must choose between them. In my view, that is a mistaken turn in his approach, despite the greatness of his work. A book can be mistaken in certain respects and still be important, still be a book one might be glad to have written or read, and, at least in my view, *Agape and Eros* is such a book.

Nevertheless, it is worth our asking whether we can do a little more than simply set in opposition to each other these two ways of describing grace—whether, that is, we can to some extent reconcile them and make place for each in Christian thinking about the moral life. Surely we should hope that we can; for without both approaches we cannot say everything that we need to say—or that St. Paul said—about the Christian life. To illustrate this we can look briefly at two very influential Christian writings: St.

Augustine's *Confessions* and Martin Luther's treatise, "The Freedom of a Christian."

"You are the doctor and I am sick," Augustine writes. His story is one of healing, of his divided will made whole by the grace of Christ working within him. It is a story of the long and winding journey of a sinner back to God, a journey in which, even when he did not always realize it, he was being drawn and empowered by grace. But there is a surprising twist to Augustine's telling. After recounting the story of his life and dramatic commitment to Christ, Augustine turns in Book 10 of the *Confessions* to taking stock of what we might call his post-conversion life. How well is he doing in his attempt to live out this commitment? Is he making progress in virtue, living in a manner that is truly marked by the grace of Christ working in him? Perhaps even to his own surprise Augustine concludes that this question cannot be satisfactorily answered. He cannot really judge whether he is making progress in this new life, whether he is growing in virtue. Why not? Because we cannot see ourselves whole, cannot see ourselves as we truly are.

Augustine examines himself, considering various sins that might tempt him. Is he drawn to gluttony? Well, then, he can fast for a time and see whether he can do without the food he desires. Is he subject to sexual temptation? Well, then, he can abstain from sexual activity and consider whether he is making progress in controlling those desires. Is he tempted to gossip or moved by curiosity to attend the spectacles at the Games? Once again, he can do without these objects of desire in order to determine how great is the hold of those desires upon him and whether he is making progress in holiness. To be sure, he may sometimes fall back into the grip of these characteristic sins; nevertheless, he is confident that the grace of God has set him on a new path. "You know," he writes, "how far you have already changed me."

But then he considers a different kind of temptation—his love of being praised. Here the task of self-examination becomes far more difficult. "For in other kinds of temptation I have at least some means of finding out about myself, but in this kind it is almost impossible." Why impossible? He can do without fine foods, give up the desire for a wife, or resign from high position, but how can he test whether he is still in the grip of an inordinate desire to be praised? How can he know that in his innermost self he cannot be happy unless he is praised by others? He could, of course, deliberately live a bad life so that others would not praise him, but that hardly seems right. He could try to make clear to others that he does not think he should be praised. But then, of course, they will praise him for that modesty. There is no test available. He cannot find a vantage point from which to see deeply enough into himself, from which to see himself whole and entire. God knows him better than he knows himself. He believes, of course, that whenever he is praised he should accept the praise not as due to him but as God's gift. "But whether this is really how I do feel I do not know. In this matter I know less of myself than of you."

Rather than looking within to see how he is progressing in the journey toward holiness, Augustine realizes that he must look to the "mediator" sent by a merciful God to share the life of sinners, so that "we may be saved through faith in His passion." That is, in those moments when we can no longer determine how we are doing in the journey back to God, those moments when we can find no way to test our progress, the direction of movement must be reversed. The God who knows us better than we know ourselves must journey to us and, in his mercy, take our side and pardon us. To say everything that needs to be said about the Christian life, Augustine had to say that.

By contrast, Luther keeps front and center grace as pardon—the God who comes in Christ to be with us. In his well-known treatise from 1520 on "The Freedom of a Christian" Luther sets out a crisp, straightforward outline for the view he will develop. First: "A Christian is a perfectly free lord of all, subject to none." Second: "A Christian is a perfectly dutiful servant of all, subject to all." And he then proceeds to develop with considerable zest the first of these assertions.

True Christian freedom, Luther writes, comes only from the pardoning grace of God enacted in Jesus. Try as we may to live in accord with God's will, what we find, he thinks, is that any honest assessment shows not success but our "inability to do good." At some moments we may do well, and some of us may seem to be better than others of us, but for all of us all of the time it will still be true that we fall short of the kind of holiness that could really please God. Anyone who is honest must, Luther writes, "despair of himself" and "seek the help which he does not find in himself elsewhere and from someone else"—namely, from the pardoning God revealed as gracious and trustworthy in Christ.

Luther proceeds at length then to praise the grace of God, who does us the "great honor" of coming to us. In one of his most well-known passages Luther underscores the way in which faith unites one with Christ "as a bride is united with her bridegroom." They now hold everything in common. Now "sins, death, and damnation will be Christ's, while grace, life, and salvation will be the soul's; for if Christ is a bridegroom, he must take upon himself the things which are his bride's and bestow upon her the things that are his." This "royal marriage" means nothing less than pardon. The bride of Christ now has the righteousness of Christ, her husband, a righteousness she may claim as her own.

Having gone on at length developing his first thesis, that a Christian is a perfectly free lord of all, Luther would now, we might expect, turn to the second thesis—that Christians are perfectly dutiful servants of others, committed to serving their needs. But he does not. Departing from the simplicity of his outline, Luther begins not with the works a Christian does for others, but with "the works which a Christian does for himself." He begins, that is, with something like a theory of the virtues, of progress in holiness. Luther cites St. Paul to the effect that this progress is "the first fruits of the Spirit," beginning steps in the long journey to become the people God intends us to be. As long as we live in this life, he writes, "we only begin to make progress in that which shall be perfected in the future life." We must discipline the body "by fastings, watchings, labors, and other reasonable discipline." Only after he has emphasized at length the necessity of such moral self-discipline does Luther finally turn to the second point in his outline—dutiful service of our neighbors.

In order to say everything he needed to say about the Christian life, Luther had to break the simplicity of his outline. He could not only speak of an immediate turn to love for neighbors by those who had been graciously pardoned. Instead, he had to write also of the power of the Spirit within us, a power that shapes and forms us to act in God-pleasing ways. "Any work," Luther concludes, "that is not done solely for the purpose of keeping the body under control or of serving one's neighbor, . . . is not good or Christian." The truth turns out to be more complicated than the outline with which he began.

Neither Augustine nor Luther could, in the end, say only one thing about the work of grace in our lives. Each had to speak of it as both power and pardon. There is both a truth of reality and a truth of experience. When we characterize grace as power—a power to cleanse our inner desires and make us holy—we point to what God is really at work doing in human history. God is graciously transforming sinners into saints—day by day, bit by bit, more and more. Our problem, of course, as Augustine realized, is that often we cannot see that this is happening in our lives. That is, experience seems to teach us a different lesson; for we do not necessarily see ourselves moving steadily along, progressing in virtue. Hence, we need not only an empowering grace that makes our lives more and more God-pleasing, but also a word of pardoning grace that returns us again and again to the simple truth that in Christ God is on our side.

No adequate Christian ethic can do without both understandings of grace. The ability to distinguish what is sometimes—perhaps often—our experience from what we believe God is at work accomplishing in history is at the heart of both moral theology and pastoral care. How these two, equally essential, languages of grace can themselves be fully reconciled as the one word of God to us in Christ is God's own end-time mystery, for the revealing of which we must patiently wait.

FOUR

Virtue and Vocation, Character and Calling

When discussing the three models of moral reasoning in Chapter One, we noted that while two of them focus chiefly on our *doing*, the third focuses more on our *being*—on the sort of person we are. Hence, that third approach can be called an ethic of character or an ethic of the virtues (and, of course, vices) that characterize us. It is worth attending a little more fully to what we mean when we speak of virtues.

In the deepest and most important sense we can think of virtues as those traits of character that fit us for life with God, that make us the sort of people who would really *want* to be in God's presence. That, after all, is what the psalmist (24:3–5) says:

> Who shall ascend the hill of the LORD?
>   And who shall stand in his holy place?
> He who has clean hands and a pure heart,
>   who does not lift up his soul to what is false,

and does not swear deceitfully.
He will receive blessing from the Lord,
and vindication from the God of his salvation.

Not just doing—clean hands that serve neighbors in love—but also being—a pure heart that loves God above all else—makes one a person who could with a whole heart desire to be in the presence of a holy God. To put it that way is to raise important theological questions, to which we will need to return before the end of this chapter. It may be useful, however, to start a little lower to the ground, considering the concept of virtue more generally.

What we mean by virtues

Trying to say what we mean by a virtue is not as straightforward as we might suppose. Probably the most useful way to describe virtues is to think of them as being rather like acquired skills. Suppose I am standing on a pitcher's mound some 60'6" away from a batter at home plate, and I throw a pitch that goes just across the outside corner of the plate at the batter's knees—perhaps the most difficult pitch to hit. The fact that I do this does not by itself show that I am a skillful pitcher. After all, my next pitch may go sailing over the catcher's head all the way to the backstop. But if, when I'm trying to, I can throw that low, outside strike time after time, I have acquired a certain skill. That ability has become habitual and engrained in me. No doubt I will not be able to do it every time I try, but, still, others will learn to depend on my ability to do it regularly.

The traits of character that we call virtues are a little like that—habits of behavior that we have acquired and, at least to some extent, mastered. They are not so much skills that are needed for just one sort of behavior (such as pitching) but needed for the whole of life. They are less like an ability to pass the written test for a driver's license than like learning to drive a car—learning to respond fittingly to whatever happens on the road. So, for example, at least since the time of Plato, prudence, justice, courage, and temperance have often been called cardinal virtues. They are always needed in life. They enable us to respond appropriately to new situations or unanticipated difficulties that we face in life.

A fuller description of the virtues will, however, require us to move beyond an example like that of the skilled baseball pitcher. We may assume that a pitcher wants to pitch effectively, even when he sometimes fails. With the virtues, however, the story is not quite the same. Sometimes I may not want to act virtuously—to be just or temperate, for example. Finding within myself contrary inclinations in need of correction, I will realize that becoming a person who can be relied upon to act virtuously will by no means be easy. In fact, it may sometimes be easier to become a person whose habits of behavior are vicious rather than virtuous.

Thus, part of the reason we need to become virtuous is a somewhat negative one: to correct our sinful inclinations. But even that does not tell the whole story. Put more positively, the virtues describe what human beings at their best can be. They mark people for whom virtuous activity has become habitual, people who can be depended on to act in certain ways—who, in the psalmist's language are characterized by clean hands and pure hearts.

This more positive understanding of virtue has very deep roots in the Western moral tradition. Aristotle begins his *Nicomachean Ethics* by asking a simple question: What is it that everyone seeks. His answer, *eudaimonia*, is a word for which there may be no perfect English translation. It means something like happiness or fulfillment—to be what human beings at their very best would be.

The next question, of course, is: What will fulfill me as a human being, what will really help me to flourish? To which Aristotle replies: Living virtuously. The virtues are excellences of character that are needed to live the kind of life that will truly fulfill us. Put more in the language of Christian faith, virtues are the traits needed to attain the vision of God. It is, as Jesus says, the pure in heart who will see God.

Who we are, what our character is like, determines what we can see. What a just person sees as an occasion for sharing with others an unjust person may see as an occasion for hoarding. What I see as lovable depends upon the sort of person I am. And so, in the end, without virtue, without the purity of heart of which Jesus and the psalmist speak, no one can see God.

Theological worries about a focus on virtue

What may seem straightforward is actually quite complicated, however, and there are at least two reasons why we might worry about a focus on virtue. Think first about how we acquire the virtues. Just as the pitcher learning to throw that low, outside strike consistently must practice it time after time, so also acquiring the virtues requires habituation over time. Only in that way can we become people who may be counted on to act justly, temperately, or humbly—not just sporadically, but regularly. It takes training for us really to possess such traits of character, to become people who habitually act virtuously.

True as this standard account of the process of acquiring the virtues is, putting it that way points to a theological problem. The novelist Christopher Beha clearly put his finger on the problem in an interview describing his return to the Roman Catholic faith (that he had left at an earlier point in life). "You can decide 'It's going to be good for my children if I raise them within the church,' or 'It's going to be good for me if I display the outer signs of belief,' but those are obviously something very, very different [from actually believing]. What needs to happen for one who has lost faith or did not ever have faith is a turning. A turning of the heart."[8]

The need for that "turning" points to something that goes deeper than the kind of habituation in virtue described by Aristotle. Every theory of the virtues, even those that are not particularly concerned with theological issues, will face this difficulty. How do I become virtuous? The standard answer is: by acting virtuously and thereby cultivating in myself the habit of virtuous behavior. That cannot really be a completely satisfactory answer, however. After all, Aristotle's complete description of acquiring virtues through habituation goes like this: "Acts are called just and self-controlled when they are the kind of acts which a just or self-controlled man would perform; but the just and self-controlled man is not he who performs these acts, but he who also performs them in the way just and self-controlled men do."

Thus, there is a paradox right at the heart of any ethic of character. In order to become virtuous I must do virtuous deeds *in the way* (with the spirit and the motivation) that a virtuous person does such deeds. But were I able to do this, I would already be virtuous, not in need of a process of habituation. It seems, then, that I cannot become virtuous unless I already am! There is no straightforward way to get from practicing virtuous deeds to becoming a virtuous person. As C. S. Lewis put it (in *Mere Christianity*), "there is a difference between doing some particular just or temperate action and being a just or temperate man." What is needed in addition is a certain quality of character that goes beyond the action itself—Beha's turning of the heart.

That is the problem—and the mystery—of all moral education. "Train up a child in the way he should go," Proverbs says, "and when he is old he will not depart from it." Yet, of course, some children do depart from it. Habituation alone is by no means foolproof. Perhaps grace, which is always a mystery and a gift that cannot be demanded, is needed. Not a grace that works like magic, but an empowering divine grace that, when and where the Spirit of Christ wills (as Jesus said to Nicodemus), gradually transforms us into people who genuinely long to be in God's presence.

There is a second, equally important theological angle, from which we might worry about a focus on becoming virtuous. The word 'focus' is, in fact, precisely the problem. It suggests the way in which serious attention to one's character directs our attention inward rather than to the task at hand. If we take seriously Jesus' framing of the two great love commands, the moral life should be directed not inward but outward toward love of God and our neighbors. There can, in fact, be something paralyzing about constant attention to oneself—constant taking of our spiritual temperature, as we sometimes say. We cannot deny the importance of character, of praying that the empowering grace of God will cultivate within us the virtues needed to live well. But freedom from attention to the self is also needed, lest our awareness of the needs of others never escapes from awareness of our own awareness. A pitcher who focuses single-mindedly on the "mechanics" of his delivery may actually tie himself in knots, becoming unable to engage effortlessly in his craft. Few great pitchers ever worked harder than Tom Seaver to master that craft, but consider the fluid grace, the loss of self, captured in Roger Angell's memory of watching Seaver pitch: "the motionless assessing pause on the hill while the sign is delivered, the easy, rocking shift of weight onto the back leg, the upraised arms, and then the left shoulder coming forward as the whole body drives forward and drops suddenly downward—down so low that the right knee scrapes the sloping dirt of the mound in an immense thrusting stride, and the right arm coming over blurrily and still flailing, even as the ball, the famous fastball, flashes across the plate, chest-high on the batter and already past his low, late swing."[9]

Living with that kind of seemingly effortless freedom will require a great deal of practice. But habituation alone, even training in virtue empowered by the grace of God, may not always be sufficient to free us from that paralyzing turn inward. For such freedom, something different—a grace that is pardon, a grace that frees us to hear the call of God—may sometimes be needed.

Vocation as God's call

Just such a sense, that true virtue requires a kind of unself-conscious spontaneity that is not an achievement but a gift, led the Protestant Reformers to find new meaning and importance in the concept of vocation. The meaning they found, however, differs in several ways from what we often mean today when we speak of vocation.

The word comes from a Latin term (*vocare*) that means "to call," or "to summon." And, of course, if there is a calling, it would seem that there must be a Caller. Today, however, the language of vocation has been turned in another direction. We may suppose that the way to find one's vocation is to ask, "what do I want to do with my life?" First I must figure out who I am, and then I will know what God calls me to be and to do. But putting it that way makes it seem as if God's call must primarily be in service of my wants—in which case it is no longer really a summons. A vocation as the Reformers understood it works the other way round. I know who I am only when I know what God calls me to be.

We have also come to think of vocations as something more like jobs—work for which we are paid, work by which we make a living. For the Reformers, however, there were important callings—to be a father or mother, to be a student—that were not ways of making a living. Rather, they were places in life where God gives us tasks to carry out and others to serve—an understanding captured well in Fred Pratt Green's hymn, "How clear is our vocation, Lord, when once we heed your call."

This understanding of the call of God goes somewhat beyond the usual understanding in the Bible, where it most often refers to God's calling of a people (Israel, or the Church). Or it may have in mind the way God can call particular persons to exercise some special function for the good of that people. Thus, Israel—and then later the Church—is called to be a people holy to God. Prophets are called to speak for God to Israel, as in the New Testament particular Christians are given different gifts that suit them for different forms of service within the body of believers. At one point, however, St. Paul uses the term in a different way that turned out to be influential in later Christian history. "Let every one," he writes in I Corinthians 7:17, "lead the life which the Lord has assigned to him, and in which God has called him." Here Paul does connect the call to be a Christian with the call to work of some sort—and not only work within the Christian community. The tasks we carry out in everyday life are given the kind of spiritual significance more usually reserved for the calling to follow Christ. Thus, those tasks can become part of one's calling from God. What we may think of simply as secular life and work can be sanctified and become part of our response to the call of God.

We may rightly say, therefore, that the calling is a gift from God, a gift that frees us from the tendency to focus on ourselves, our spiritual condition, our accomplishments, our virtue. It is the gift that works in us that needed "turning." We are freed to focus on the needs of others and liberated from the attempt to know our character fully, freed from the sort of attempt that Augustine came to see is doomed to fail. This sense of freedom for the tasks given us in everyday life is beautifully expressed in George Herbert's poem, "The Elixir."[10] Herbert, an Anglican priest and a great seventeenth-century poet, plays with the medieval alchemists' search for some potion or elixir—the philosopher's stone—that would turn other metals into gold. The poem reads in part:

> Teach me my God and King
> In all things thee to see,
> And what I do for anything,
> To do it as for thee.
>
> . . . .
>
> A servant with this clause
> Makes drudgery divine;
> Who sweeps a room, as for thy laws,
> Makes that and th' action fine.
>
> This is the famous stone
> That turneth all to gold:
> For that which God doth touch and own
> Cannot for less be told.

When they are drawn into our vocation, therefore, the tasks God sets before us daily are no longer simply ways to care for ourselves and for others close to us. Sanctified by God's summons, they are the places where God calls us to live out the freedom given us in Christ.

Theological Worries about Vocation

George Herbert's poem is beautiful, and its vision of the beauty in honest work done in response to God's call has had a powerful impact in the history of our culture; nevertheless, we should worry about sanctifying drudgery, especially when it is others' drudgery. Some work is backbreaking and dangerous. Some work is tedious and boring. To be sure, that sort of work may sometimes be our calling and will need to be done as part of our service to others. But we should not characterize it in ways that may sound almost unbelievable to those who actually do it—as if they should seek out more time for such work rather than escape it if they can. So there are reasons to be cautious when we use the language of vocation.

Even when we use this language carefully, however, there is a second reason for worry. The language of vocation can have effects we might not have anticipated. The point of honoring our callings is to remind us that there is a second great love commandment. Not only are we to love God with all that is in us, we are also to serve the needs of our neighbors. That is why we sanctify everyday life, understanding our seemingly mundane and secular tasks as holy. Finding our vocation in these tasks underscores the truth that we do not have to escape from the world into some distinctively religious sphere in order to please God.

True as this may be, it is also true that this understanding of vocation can have exactly the opposite effect. That is, it can have a secularizing effect, if we begin to suppose that God's sanctifying of our ordinary work leaves everything in the world just as it is and in no way transforms the work of our callings. Then, as Dietrich Bonhoeffer once put it, the justification of the sinner in the world becomes the justification of sin and the world. In that case, it will soon seem, there may be no difference between a carpenter and a

Christian carpenter, a father and a Christian father, a historian and a Christian historian, a soldier and a Christian soldier, an artist and a Christian artist. What they do is exactly the same. It's just, we may come to think, that the Christian does it all with a different "spirit."

We are then well on our way to making the call of God largely irrelevant. Understanding what we do as our vocation is not supposed to be a reason for leaving the task just as we found it. God never lets us rest content in our callings. When God summons us, he calls us to the work, but he also calls us out from it to himself—to greater perfection and holiness. Inevitably that must mean transformation not only of the worker but also of the work. Attention to the work to which we are called by the second great command does not eliminate the command to love God with heart, soul, mind, and strength. Attention to the demands of vocation does not eliminate the need to grow in virtue. It is all too easy for us to suppose that attention to our calling—to service of neighbors in everyday life—is all that God asks of us. And if we begin to think in that way, it is unlikely that the work we do will really be transformed by the call of God.

Finally, there is at least one more reason for caution when we think about vocation. We may sometimes picture our response to God's call as if it were automatic or spontaneous. In grace God calls us to be his people, assures us that we are on his side, frees us from self-concern, and thereby frees us to respond to the call to serve others. We just seem to know what needs doing and are eager to do it. But the Christian life is not quite that simple. Virtue is also needed.

It is one thing to be eager to serve the needs of our neighbors. It is another to be the sort of person who is actually likely to do them much good, a person characterized by virtuous habits of behavior that allow us truly to see what serves their well-being. Only those whose character has been well formed can really see the truth of things. Earlier we noted that an emphasis on virtue could have the unfortunate effect of turning our gaze entirely inward, locking us in self-concern. Now, though, we must note the other side of that coin. Without the discipline of a character shaped by virtuous habits, all our concern for others may not genuinely discern and serve their well-being.

If we attend only to the disciplines that form a virtuous character, or only to the vocation for which God frees us, we will not really have entered into the complexities of the Christian life—a life moved by the Spirit of Christ and structured in virtue by that same Spirit.

FIVE

The Church's Authority to Teach

When Dietrich Bonhoeffer wrote, "the Body of Christ takes up space on earth," he was underscoring the truth that the church has its own culture, which structures the life of believers.[11] To live within the church means, therefore, to be shaped and constrained by its way of life and its disciplines. Yet, of course, the church is not immune to a certain kind of tension that arises within any community—a tension between the authority of the community and the desire of individuals freely to shape their lives in the world.

Nothing is more common in life than such tension. From individual citizens who must set aside their own desires and obey laws they may think unwise, to athletes who must subordinate their individual talents to a coach's plan that may seem to undervalue their possibilities, versions of this tension confront us constantly. No doubt the problem is especially intense, however, when the final authority of the community to which we belong is truly *final*—when that *author*ity is the *author* of our being. Thus, for example, the Jewish philosopher Michael Wyschogrod writes:

> Must the believing Jew sacrifice his conscience in obedience to God? Must he give up an ultimate individuality when he embraces the covenant which is more national than individual and must he . . . reject the Kierkegaardian single one for a relation with God that is always social and in which the ultimate aloneness before God yields to the community of Israel which is ruled by law rather than conscience? . . . Perhaps conscience is the Isaac in each one of us, which, though we love, we must be prepared to offer on the altar of divine sacrifice.[12]

Although this may be a general problem for religious believers, here we can approach it as a specifically Christian question that must work itself out within the life of the church. The tension between freedom and authority in the church's life is not a single problem but several different problems intertwined. Here we can consider just a few aspects of the tension.

Authority and Freedom

Especially since the time of the Enlightenment, the church's authority to structure the lives of its members has come to seem problematic. To allow ourselves to be governed by "oughts" pronounced by an authoritative church may seem inauthentic, may seem to diminish the importance of human freedom, and may be too closely tied to a particular community's way of life and, hence, seem insufficiently universal. Insofar as Christian thinkers have accepted that Enlightenment critique, the only role left for the church to play in our moral life is that of motivator. The church is needed to help motivate people to fulfill their moral duties (whose ground and authority, however, lie in reason rather than in the revelation to which the church is appointed to witness). But a cheerleader is not the same as an authority.

Consider a realm of life other than the church in which we encounter authority. Why should a son honor and obey his father? Suppose I say, "I follow my father's instruction because I find his advice to be intelligent and wise." Is that *obeying* my father? Acknowledging his *authority*? Or is it doing what I myself think wise, while nodding decorously in the direction of my father?

In a short but characteristically challenging piece titled, "Of the Difference Between a Genius and an Apostle," Søren Kierkegaard writes, "to honour one's father because he is intelligent is impiety." That is, it is not the *pietas* a son owes his father; it is simply taking note of the fact that the father's views reduplicate the son's. Hence, Kierkegaard notes, it is impossible to "obey" on the basis of one's judgment that one's father is correct. For similar reasons, he suggests, the Genius and the Apostle are qualitatively different.

Consider the proposition, "there is eternal life." This might, Kierkegaard notes, be spoken by Christ; it might also be spoken by a theological student. Each says the same thing, and the proposition is no more profound in the mouth of one than the other. "And yet there is an eternal qualitative difference between them." The two statements do not become equal in authority simply because they are equally insightful and profound—or, for that matter, equally commonplace. Or, again, although for Christians the letters of St. Paul teach authoritatively, "as a genius St. Paul cannot be compared with either Plato or Shakespeare, as a coiner of beautiful similes he comes pretty low down in the scale, as a stylist his name is quite obscure—and as an upholsterer: well, I frankly admit I have no idea how to place him."

The possibility that I might be appointed to exercise apostolic authority in the church is not dependent on my talents, my theological training or profundity, my feeling that this is what I ought to do—by any of "the possibilities" my high school guidance counselor may have discerned in me. One becomes an Apostle only by God's appointment and exercises apostolic authority for that reason alone.

If this is true, however, its implications for how we ought to live are surely troubling. The church teaches with authority—that is, it unfolds for us the truth about a world created and redeemed by God, the whole counsel of God about how we are to live. But this teaching may sometimes or often seem more like arbitrary command than wise counsel—as, for example, when it is inadequately articulated; when it seems to leave important questions unanswered; when it does not cohere with our own best and most serious attempt to think through the matters being taught; or, perhaps most disturbing, when it seems remote from our own desires, when it seems almost unconcerned with our happiness or fulfillment in life.

Our problem, then, is an intricate one, and I will not claim to solve it so much as to explore it. The church both *states* its teaching and *argues* for it. Indeed, as William Werpehowski once suggested to me, we might say that to *state* church teaching without also *arguing* for it is not sufficiently to *teach*. Yet, the very need to argue seems to undermine the church's authority to state its teaching, while simple statement without accompanying argument may not seem helpful.

I can illustrate this by noting what has often been my own experience when reading papal encyclicals. (I say this, of course, as a Lutheran, not a Roman Catholic; yet, the problem might be still more intense for one obligated in a way I am not to give encyclicals considerable deference.) The *genre* of the encyclical has often seemed inadequate to me, for it states church teaching more than it offers a rationale for that teaching. And, in fact, the most interesting encyclical letter I have ever read—*Veritatis Splendor*—is interesting precisely because, unlike so many others, it offers a long and sustained moral argument. It seeks—uncharacteristically—not merely to state church teaching but to argue for it. Yet, in so doing, it invites the sort of reading one is more inclined to give the Genius than the Apostle—it invites the observation that it is "interesting" or "worth pondering."

Suppose we think of just a few examples from the realm of sexual and reproductive ethics, where the tension between freedom and authority in the church's life has often seemed quite pronounced, at least in recent years: (1) a Christian woman who is pregnant but abandoned by the father of their child and who feels that her life will spiral out of control if she completes the pregnancy and gives birth to her child; (2) a man, regular in church attendance, trapped for years in an unhappy marriage, but drawn now toward a woman at work with whom he seems to find the happiness that has been missing from his life for so long; (3) a young Christian man drawn by a powerful desire for sexual intimacy with another man, sensing here the answer to a longing that has been buried deep within him; (4) a married couple at risk for serious genetic disease, who want children, but children free of that disease, and who think that preimplantation genetic diagnosis—to select out and eliminate at-risk embryos—is the way to fulfill their desire for healthy children.

The church—when witnessing faithfully to the will of God—teaches with authority that the pregnant woman should not abort her child, that the married man should not divorce his wife and marry another whose companionship promises more happiness, that the young man drawn toward genital intimacy with another of his own sex ought not satisfy that desire, and that the married couple who desire healthy children must understand that children—and, especially, children of a particular sort—are not our entitlement, and that it is wrong to destroy nascent human life for eugenic reasons.

Perhaps, though, in any or all of these cases, devout believers will not understand why the church teaches as it does—what sense its teaching makes. Perhaps, even, they will sometimes experience this teaching as a sharp blow that wounds them deeply. They may be tempted, then, to think of the church not as an authority but as, shall we say, a "moral resource," whose counsel is to be considered along with counsel from other quarters. How, in such circumstances, is the church to teach with authority, seeking to unfold the shape of a life that follows Christ?

We should not be too quick to suppose that the church can teach with authority only when it declares or commands, only by exercising a kind of quasi-political authority that simply requires certain behavior as a condition of membership. There may, we must acknowledge, come a time for such exercise of authority, though that will always be an occasion for regret. But the church's authority is exercised not only in commanding but *also and first* through rich and expansive teaching—in studying together the scriptural revelation and its theological tradition, in seeking to grow in understanding through critical reflection and analysis. This reflection must include what we might call an ecumenism of time—according to which the voices heard are not only those of our own time but also, and especially, those of the great teachers of the church in centuries past, from whom we still seek to learn.

We begin with such reflection rather than with unadorned statement or political command for the simple—but crucial—reason that the church not only speaks God's word but also hears that word, is addressed by it, and compelled to reflect upon it. The church is Christ's body, to be sure, but these two—Christ and his Body—are not mystically fused; for Christ is also Lord over that Body. Challenges to the church's teaching are not, therefore, simply denounced and rejected, though, again, we must acknowledge that a time may come when that needs to happen. Challenges are heard, examined, studied, refined—all in the hope that, even if unacceptable in many respects, they may contain a part of the truth, which can then be opened up in fuller and richer ways.

It is, though, a *sine qua non* of faithful, churchly reflection and thinking that, while the church hears and examines a challenge to its teaching, none of us thinks himself or herself free to act as if the challenge had already been accepted and approved. To live within the church and—with a freedom given by the Holy Spirit—to acknowledge the church's authority, is something very different from being a free-floating philosopher of the moral life, answerable only to one's own critical judgment.

At any rate, the church seeks first to help us understand how our duty may become our delight, how the command of God does not so much tell us what we *ought* to do as, rather, directs us to the only kind of life that can ultimately allow us to flourish as human beings: a life lived with rather than against the grain of the universe God has created. The purpose of the church's reflection and teaching is that we come to see and believe that God's command does not destroy us but perfects and completes us. There are, of course, mysteries—at times painful ones—hidden within that perfecting. This perfecting is, as Josef Pieper once wrote:

> one of those concepts which probably can never be known and defined before it is experienced. It is simply in the nature of the thing that the apprentice can have no specific idea of what the perfection of mastery looks like from inside or of all that is going to be demanded of him. Perfection always includes transformation. And transformation necessarily means parting from what must be overcome and abandoned precisely for the sake of preserving identity in change.

That transformation may even resemble "passing through something akin to dying." It is, therefore, Pieper hauntingly suggests, "much more than an innocuous piety when Christendom prays, 'Kindle in us the fire of thy love.'"[13]

There is no instruction book that can tell us when the church's attempt to argue or explain its teaching has not succeeded and the time has come simply for unadorned statement of and insistence upon that teaching. There are no rules specifying how we know that the church's attempt to unfold the counsel of God has, to our regret, failed to achieve its desired end. No voice from heaven will tell us that, now, the integrity of the church's shared life requires that obedience be asked even of those who still feel themselves unable to make sense of the church's teaching.

But we may come to such a point—and not only with respect to dogmatic matters of "faith" but also with respect to matters of moral "life." For, in fact, these matters are tightly interwoven. Think again of the examples from sexual and reproductive ethics that I used earlier to illustrate our experience of a tension between freedom and authority. In various ways they invite us to reflect upon the meaning of our embodiment and our creation as male and female. We are tempted to suppose that our "real" self is separate from and transcends the sexually differentiated body—and that this real self uses the body to satisfy our desires and achieve our purposes.

That way of thinking is a version of the first heresy the church ever faced, which thought of salvation as deliverance from the body. And in the face of that temptation the church had to find ways to bear witness to the truth that Jesus of Nazareth was God incarnate, and that, because Jesus had risen from the grave, Christians too should await the resurrection of their bodies. Those Christological and Trinitarian dogmatic beliefs, whose authority we acknowledge and which could hardly be altered without destroying the integrity of the church's shared life, are in fact closely related to what we teach in sexual ethics about the significance of our embodiment. Faith and life are deeply intertwined, and the church cannot be faithful unless it structures its life in a way that coheres with the faith it proclaims.

Thus, if the church is to be itself and freely to shape its own life in obedience to its Lord, it will eventually have to distinguish between those who heed its teaching and seek to follow Christ and those who—even if they continue to think of themselves as believers—will not heed that teaching or follow that path of discipleship. Freedom to determine one's being is not just for individuals. Communities also must be free to determine who and what they are. After all, the Body of Christ takes up space on earth. This is space for preaching the gospel and for administering the sacraments, but it is also space in which believers may order their shared life—the life of the Body—in accord with the will of God to which the church witnesses. This means, of necessity, that the church must exercise authority over the lives of individual believers.

And if one of those individual believers cannot or will not hear in the church's voice the voice of the Lord? If one feels that to obey the teaching of the church would violate the responsibility he has as an individual before God, would compel him to deny the gospel as he understands it? What then? This is, no doubt, the most painful question of all, and it arises inevitably out of the train of thought I have been pursuing. I note it here in order, for the moment, to set it aside. I will eventually return to it, though I cannot promise any neat resolution. Before even attempting that, however, we do well to think about a second aspect of the tension between freedom and authority.

Forming Character: From Inside or Outside?

How do members of Christ's Body become people who can—without simply bowing to authority—freely take up the way of life authoritatively taught by the church? We sometimes think—indeed, we like to think—that such obedience is and can only be our free response to the gospel. That gospel renews our spirit and, in so doing, also reorders the structure of our lives. Transformation happens from the inside out. Renewed inwardly by the Spirit of Christ, we are enabled to hear with receptive hearts the church's instruction about how we ought to live.

It may be worth reflecting upon the fact that few parents think that way when struggling to raise their children. They worry about where their children go to school, about who their playmates and peers are, about the ways they use their free time, about what they see on television or the internet. They anticipate that the daily habits of their children's lives will help to shape their inner spirit—not perfectly or inevitably, of course, but nonetheless powerfully. They worry about all these things because they know that Aristotle was, at least to some extent, right in saying that moral virtue is habit long continued. The inner spirit is shaped and formed from the outside, by the structures and disciplines within which we live. Most parents look for ways to let their children know they love them and trust them to do what is best, but most also think it would be foolhardy to do nothing more than announce such trust, paying no attention to the schools their children attend, the friends with whom they play, the computer games that occupy their time, and so forth. Thus, for example, a mother who schools her children at home writes that the various aspects of their study are "elements in an integrated whole from which, we hope and pray, our children will emerge one day so firmly formed that nothing in this world can unbend them."

Perhaps so. But even the best formation cannot guarantee the desired result, and one hopes she takes seriously that this is a matter for hope and prayer. Too much confidence here would be a mistake—and, in fact, a theological mistake. What father wants to take full responsibility for shaping the character—much less the soul—of his child? What mother does not understand that her child's inner spirit is free and cannot simply be molded, however strenuous her efforts? Only God can bear such responsibility. There are limits to what we can accomplish working from the outside in, though, to be sure, we must attempt it.

Something similar is true of the church's authoritative shaping of the lives of believers. Although the church is the Body of Christ that takes up space in the world, although it is an extension of the incarnation, its disciplined way of life cannot programmatically guarantee to elicit the free obedience of its members. That is why in baptism we hand our children over to God, acknowledging that only he can finally stand as guarantor of their faith. The limit to the church's authority to form the spiritual lives of its members lies in a truth noted earlier—namely, that the church too is addressed by the Word of God. It truly is Christ's Body, but, at the same time,

Christ stands over against it exercising his Lordship. It must listen in obedience and only then speak in the name of its Lord.

That the church's power to form and shape us is limited is, therefore, a truth never to be forgotten. But we would be badly mistaken to stop there and say no more than that. What sort of creatures would we be if the church's structures and disciplines were no more than a moral resource, if they had no authority to shape our lives in God-pleasing ways? We would be virtual angels, entirely free spirits—bodiless beings not located in any particular time and place, immune to the influence of other people or institutions. That cannot be right. We do not, in fact, form our hearts to obey only as single individuals. Although Christ calls each of us as individuals, that call is a call to belong—a call to community in the fellowship of the church.

It is almost always a mistake, therefore, to begin by setting ourselves—as purportedly free and autonomous spirits—over against an authoritative church. The very freedom we have to follow Christ is one that has been nurtured in us by the church. Our powers of judgment, our capacity to discern what is the will of God, our ability to understand the counsel of God—all this has been formed in us as members of the church. The inner spirit with which we freely offer our obedience to God is the spirit of a human being, one who is located in space and time, one for whom the body is the place of personal presence—one whose free obedience, therefore, can and must be taught, nurtured, and shaped by the church.

But also—and here I return at last to the question I left dangling earlier—one whose faith and obedience are shaped by the church's Lord. The church is addressed—corporately, as a body—by its Lord; it shapes its members in accord with that address; but each believer is also addressed singly. That is, each believer is addressed not only by the Body of Christ but also by the Head of that Body, the Lord himself. No matter how closely shared our lives are, no matter how true it is that we have been baptized into a new fellowship, we cannot finally confess or repent or believe for each other. Before God each of us is that "single individual" with whom Kierkegaard was so obsessed, and it is not even wrong to say that we are obligated—or, if you prefer, freed—to assess the church's teaching and instruction for ourselves, listening prayerfully to the Word of God revealed in Jesus and testified to in the Scriptures.

Indeed, it is necessary that individual Christians have such freedom. Because the church is not mystically fused with Christ, any particular claim to ecclesiastical authority may be mistaken or inauthentic. To be sure, there can never come a time when the world is abandoned by the risen Christ and his authentic voice is not heard in and through the church, but that does not relieve us of the need to judge for ourselves whether on any particular occasion churchly claims to speak for God are the voice of the Master who has also addressed us singly. This is, as Oliver O'Donovan noted, the true sense in which the church can be said to be invisible, and it may be that "the believer must, in the logic of discipleship, behave 'as though' he or she were alone, as though all the rest had fled as they fled from Christ in Gethsemane."[14]

We should make this point only with great care, not forgetting that even the individual who must do his own judging has learned what that means and its importance within the community of the church. There is a kind of "hyper-Protestantism"—more exactly, I suspect, a form of Enlightenment rationality—that turns first rather than last to this notion of the single individual and is unwilling to recognize a place for the church to speak with authority. To do that, however, is really to say that there is no apostolic authority, but only the special insight of the genius.

Even if we avoid that mistaken understanding of the priesthood of all believers, however, there is a sense in which we should say with Kierkegaard that eternity never counts. Never lumps individuals together into a sum. Before God each of us is equal—and equally, that single individual. What am I to do, then, if—even after patient conversation and reflection—the church's teaching makes no sense to me? Or seems to ask of me more than it ought? Or, even, seems to destroy the person I am rather than renew and complete me?

If the church is really a body, if it truly takes up space in the world, then it must be free to hear the Word of God and shape its life in accordance with what it hears. If I, though, am also, even as that single individual, free to hear the Word of God, what shall we say when my freedom to listen to God and the church's freedom to order its life in the manner it considers faithful seem to clash? I cannot and should not claim—whether on the basis of some notion of the priesthood of all believers or simply on the basis of a rejection of heteronomy—that the church cannot speak authoritatively to me, even if only to determine that I do not faithfully represent its teaching.

The church must be free to do that if it is to order its common life with integrity and faithfulness. And if I am simultaneously free to live immediately before God, I may have to step out from under the visible church's authority and stand apart from its common life—even if I understand that as my way of bearing witness to what I think the church ought to be. But what I cannot claim, in so doing, is the authority of the church's apostle. I may, to be sure, think myself a Genius, but then I can only speak "without authority"—to borrow for my own purposes a formula Kierkegaard used in somewhat different ways.

And then we must pray: pray that when one day we see the full meaning of the truth that God was in Christ reconciling the world to himself, the clash between these conflicting claims about the Word of God to us will be healed; and our hearts, all our hearts as one, will be freely and joyfully set to obey God's commandments.

SIX

The Way of Life and the Way of Death

In the Gospel of Mark Jesus and his disciples come out of the temple, and one of the disciples says, "Look, Teacher, what wonderful stones and what wonderful buildings!" To which Jesus replies, "There will not be left here one stone upon another, that will not be thrown down." Commenting on this exchange, John Courtney Murray (in *We Hold These Truths*) observed that even great cultural achievements may, in the end, amount to nothing. Sometimes, he noted, we seem to be caught between two ways of life—one a life of human achievement and improvement, the other a life directed entirely toward God. And the question we must ask ourselves is: Are these two ways simply and entirely opposed? Or can we somehow inhabit both?

That is a question Christians have always had to ask themselves. The *Didache*, one of the earliest post-New Testament Christian writings that we know of, contrasts "two ways"—the way of life and the way of death. And almost two thousand years later, near the end of the twentieth century, Pope John Paul II, in the encyclical letter *Evangelium Vitae*, set a "culture of life" over against a "culture of death." The clash between these two ways confronts Christians in all areas of life, though perhaps nowhere so obviously or contentiously as in political life—most obviously, for example, in the decision to use (or refuse to use) force in the service of important societal ends. In an attempt to think through this question we can turn to one of the truly seminal works in Christian social ethics: H. Richard Niebuhr's *Christ and Culture*.[15]

It would be hard to think of a book that has, over the course of the last six or seven decades, been more influential in shaping Christian social ethics. Niebuhr characterizes the Christian life in terms of a "double movement"—away from the world to God, but also from God to the world. Christians are, he writes, "forever being challenged to abandon all things for the sake of God; and forever being sent back into the world to teach and practice all the things that have been commanded them." Although Niebuhr's concern was for life within the world of culture generally, not just political activity in particular, the typology he develops in *Christ and Culture* can be especially instructive when we think about how Christians should exercise political responsibility. For example, it seems right to say—indeed, St. Paul says as much in Romans 13—that government serves human well-being. It secures some measure of peace, order, and justice in human life, and those are surely considerable goods. Yet, government does this precisely by being willing to coerce, and to use force (even sometimes lethal force). Government seems necessary and, in its own way, good; nevertheless, it often falls well short of our highest ideals. Participating in its work may sometimes give us the sense that we have dirtied our hands or corrupted our spirit. To use power even for good ends may lead us to act in ways that fall short of our own ideals; yet, adhering to our sense of what is good may seem to leave us powerless to shape life for good. Hence, Christians have always had to ask themselves how they are to be at home in a world in which they are drawn in two, seemingly opposed, directions.

The Types

Niebuhr describes five different ways Christians have responded to this question, describing the five as "typical partial answers.," and as "great *motifs* that appear and reappear." I propose first to state, in very brief form, how each of the five types might respond to the question, "Should Christians participate in government's use of force?" These depictions are mine, not Niebuhr's, but I hope they do capture at least some themes that are central to his types. Then, having outlined these five "typical partial answers" to a particular question, we can discuss them in more general detail.

Christ against Culture (radical Christians): Jesus said, "Do not resist evil." Disciples are not above their master, and Christians should expect that suffering may come when they attempt to follow Jesus. But their calling is not to take responsibility for public life. They are called to be a people faithful to Jesus and obedient to his command—a people who bear witness to an alternative way of life that seeks rigorously to keep Jesus' command not to resist evil.

Christ of Culture (cultural Christians): Christians should seek to achieve and sustain a perpetual peace among peoples. This can be accomplished only as universal reason comes to rule more and more in our common life, subduing the animal passions that bring human beings into conflict. Such peace is, in fact, the goal toward which divine providence is working through a long process of historical (and sometimes revolutionary) development.

Christ above Culture (synthesists): It is rational to seek to preserve one's life and the lives of others with whom we live. Hence, as rational creatures, Christians may do so. Nevertheless, some Christians may be called to a higher level of obedience that leads them to withdraw into more cohesive communities, not to use force, and to accept whatever suffering comes to them for Christ's sake.

Christ and Culture in Paradox (dualists): In order to serve the neighbors God has given us, Christians may sometimes need to use force. That is, they may do for the sake of others what Christ seems to forbid, accepting a life that is always drawn in two directions. They can live, therefore, only by faith—only by trusting that God forgives the sin they necessarily do.

Christ the Transformer of Culture (conversionists): Justice in public life is simply what Christian love requires when the needs of two or more neighbors conflict. In such circumstances of conflict the use of force is permitted to defend the needy, but love will still set limits to the ways in which and the circumstances under which force may justly be used. Though justice cannot simply become love, it can be shaped and reshaped over time by a love that recognizes a neighbor even in the enemy.

Niebuhr characterizes the last three of these types as belonging to the "church of the center," the broad middle of approaches to social ethics. This means, on the one hand, that the first two types really set the terms for thinking about Christians and society, while the last three may more often appeal to us precisely because they acknowledge greater complexity in public life.

The second-century Church Father Tertullian is an example of the way in which, according to Niebuhr, radical Christians tend to localize sin outside the Christian community. Tertullian depicts those who attend the Roman games and shows in the amphitheater, as "seated where there is nothing of God." Of course, it may be rather natural to characterize others as enemies of God when they, in turn, are crying "to the lions." And this should remind us that, although a typology is inevitably an abstraction, none of these types should be read too abstractly, entirely apart from the historical circumstances. This first "typical" approach to Christian social responsibility is a permanent possibility for Christians. It is not just a "type." It is fundamental Christian language. Nor need we characterize it simply as rejection of the world, even if it may sometimes seem that way. More positively, we may think of such Christians as drawn by the lure of Christ, obedient to his lordship.

Rather than thinking of two ways diverging, the second type (cultural Christians) sees history as a process in which two ways are converging. Here the kingdom of Christ is identified with cultural tasks—building the world community, civilizing the human animal. By God's providence this is happening within the history of our world. Perhaps for now some use of force remains necessary, but we can believe that a day is coming when peace will be established among the peoples of the world. It is, I think, fair to say that any reader of *Christ and Culture* will come away thinking that Niebuhr sees this type as less satisfying than any of the others. It seems to lack any sense of eschatological reservation, any sense that the kingdom of God will come not only by fulfilling historical possibilities but also by negating even the best of them. But this doesn't mean that there is nothing to be said for the cultural Christian. Saying that would imply that the gospel of Christ has no effect in history and makes little genuine difference in the lives of Christian people. But there is, after all, such a thing as a relatively Christianized culture. As Oliver O'Donovan once put it in a sentence that nicely captures the relation of these first two types: "The church must be prepared to welcome the homage of the kings when it is offered to the Lord of the martyrs."[16]

The first of the three types in the broad church of the center Niebuhr characterizes as synthesist. What is being synthesized? Roughly speaking, two distinct, but essentially harmonious, ways to live as Christians. The picture here is roughly that given its greatest articulation by St. Thomas—the medieval synthesis of what we can call (somewhat inaccurately) higher and lower forms of the Christian life. Those who have a genuinely "religious" calling—the monks, for example—seek a life of perfection, devoted wholly and entirely to God. But many other Christians, even if they do not seek that sort of perfection and may need to participate in the work of controlling and restraining evil in the world, can live a life that is rightly ordered in relation to God. And these two ways of life stand in harmonious relation; each needs the other, and they are held together within one Christian civilization. Similarly, Christians can appreciate and affirm insight into truth from wherever it comes, while still believing that something more than unaided reason is needed for true human wholeness.

One of Niebuhr's criticisms of the Christ above culture approach is really less a criticism than another indication that we could read these types too abstractly. The great nineteenth century Pope Leo XIII attempted to revive in his own time the synthetic thought of St. Thomas. Niebuhr argues, however, that Leo was not really synthesizing Christ with the culture of his time. Rather, he was commending to his contemporaries the culture of an earlier (medieval) time. And that is indeed one way to describe what the Pope was attempting. Another way to put it, however, would be to say that Leo was seeking to transform the culture of his time, to move it in a more thoroughly Christian direction. Thus, a synthesist who lived in Leo's time and place perhaps inevitably became more like a conversionist (Niebuhr's fifth type).

An even deeper issue—namely, the flirtation with relativism that appears and reappears within Niebuhr's writing—is also important in his evaluation of the synthesist approach so characteristic of Roman Catholicism. Refusing to identify God with any historical event or achievement, he says of synthesists: "The effort to bring Christ and culture, . . . the temporal and the eternal, . . . into one system of thought and practice tends, perhaps inevitably, to the absolutizing of what is relative, the reduction of the infinite to a finite form." But then, what shall we say about belief in the incarnation, belief that the infinite God has taken our finite human nature into his own life? Likewise, the presence of the risen Christ in the bread and wine of the Lord's Supper could, on Niebuhr's terms only be understood as another instance of "absolutizing" what is finite, believing that the infinite God is present among us. To be sure, Leo XIII may be wrong and Niebuhr right, but it is evident here that the typology seems to reject beliefs that would be central to the synthesist position.

Those Niebuhr characterizes as dualists experience Christ and culture in paradox (though it is not always clear what "paradox" means here). In some respects they are not far from the first type, the radical Christian. They too know that what the world sometimes seems to require of us Christ may seem to forbid and that, therefore, these two spheres of our life often appear to clash. The dualist differs from the radical Christian simply—but significantly—in believing that, because both worlds are God's, he commands us to live within both. And that, of course, might be said to be paradoxical. The crucial question for the dualist, particularly when we consider the use of force, is how one can have a good conscience when doing what Jesus seems to forbid. All we can do then is cling in faith to the promise that for Christ's sake God is still well pleased with us. The problem, of course, is that this seems to make faith entirely an inner trust, compatible with acting in ways that seem contrary to the lordship of Christ.

The tension between a dualist's two ways may sometimes seem to go so deep that we have a hard time affirming that both worlds are God's. Is it really just two ways within the one world that is God's, the whole of it his redeemed creation? Or has the commitment to dualism and paradox gone so deep into the theological system that we seem to have two gods, not the one God revealed in Christ? If so, the tension would actually no longer exist and the term "paradoxical" would no longer be apt. For then we would seem committed to doing evil, to serving some god other than the one revealed in Jesus. But Christian faith must in the end affirm, as St. Paul says in 2 Corinthians, that in the God revealed in Christ "it is always yes," not yes and no.

Niebuhr does, however, give his readers a very helpful clue about how best to understand what is "paradoxical" in the dualist's approach. "It sounds paradoxical," he writes at one point, "because the effort is being made to state in a monologue a meaning that is only clear in the dramatic encounters and re-encounters of God and the souls of men." That is, what the dualist offers is less a theological system than the report of an experience—an experience any serious believer is likely to have from time to time when setting his highest ideals over against the seeming necessities of everyday life. Understood in this way, the Christ and culture in paradox motif offers profound insight into the tensions of Christian life, even though taken alone it will hardly tell us whether or when an action like the use of force is right and appropriate. Such action may preserve human life toward the kingdom of God, but it cannot in itself help to build that kingdom.

Those whom Niebuhr calls "conversionists" believe, as do the dualists, that Christians live in two somewhat opposed worlds. But these worlds are not simply opposed, nor simply in tension with each other. For if these worlds are God's, and if there is only one God (the gracious God in whom it is always "yes"), we must seek to bring them into a relation that acknowledges the lordship of Christ. That means we must be constantly seeking to transform the structures of our world, bringing them ever more into conformity with the mind of Christ. Hence, for conversionists there is a constant dynamic movement in the Christian life. Nothing in human history is yet in final form, and whatever our cultural circumstances, they are still in need of further conversion while the history of redemption continues.

Unlike the synthesists, conversionists believe that everything in our natural life is distorted until brought into proper relation to God. But unlike the dualists, conversionists do not think that the tension between the way of life and the way of death is static in human life. On the contrary, history is a history of redemption, and we can have some confidence that a truly Christian spirit can permeate and transform the world's structures. Therefore, when we look at the world, we should not see simply corruption that, at best, can be held in check. We should see a good creation gone awry, needing to be redirected toward and transformed into the kingdom of Christ.

The question we must ask of conversionists is whether they have truly retained the fundamental Christian sense—present from St. Paul and the *Didache* up to Pope John Paul II—that we live in a world in which two ways diverge. If not, then this type could easily lose its orientation toward an eschatological future and collapse into a new version of the second type (the cultural Christian)—a fate, of course, that Niebuhr himself would have regretted.

Taking Stock

Paul Ramsey did not hesitate to write that "everywhere" in Niebuhr's writings it is plain that he belongs to the "Christ the Transformer of Culture" type.[17] This seems right. Many have noted that, despite what Niebuhr says, the typology is not really neutral. That, of course, need not be a problem, and we should be open to the possibility that one of the types may display more of the truth than do the others. About that question, however, Niebuhr, despite his leanings, was not always clear—in part because of his relativist tendencies. We need clarity about an important distinction. Is each of the types "partly true" (and, hence, also "partly false")? Or does each of the types open to us "part of the truth" (in which case it need not also be partly false, even if in some ways incomplete)?

More generally, it is worth noting again that typologies do not always give us a clear sense of historical movement or development. Perhaps, as I noted earlier, a synthesist who finds himself in a time and place in which Christian faith is on the margins of the culture may begin to seem more like a conversionist. And likewise, someone theoretically attached to the Christ transforming culture type may sound more like a synthesist if he finds himself in a time and place where Christian faith has to some extent succeeded in shaping the culture. And, of course, if we find ourselves in a time and place when the church is on the margins of the culture, or even where the culture is actively hostile to Christian belief, we may learn once again to say: "There are two ways in conflict, and we must choose between them." In a sense that is always true, of course; we are always drawn in two directions. But there are times and places when it cannot *not* be said. And although cultural Christianity may be the most theologically defective of the types, we should still be grateful if we live in a time and place where the culture has been shaped into a closer approximation to Christ's kingdom.

Finally, it is worth noting once again, as Niebuhr well knew, that the greatest of Christian thinkers are unlikely to fit neatly into any single one of the types. Consider St. Augustine (considered under Niebuhr's conversionist type) and Luther (clearly belonging to Niebuhr's dualist type).

One of the most powerful passages Augustine ever wrote (in *City of God*, 19.6) depicts the plight of a philosopher judge—a public official who, in order to carry out his duty to seek the truth, must approve very questionable practices, even torture. (And we should not forget that as a Bishop Augustine was himself a public official.) Should such an official resign his position? Withdraw from public life? No, Augustine famously answers. Tempting as that might be, he would then fail in his duties toward those he serves in his office. So he must do what his office requires while praying, "deliver me from my necessities." At such a moment Augustine, conversionist though he may often be, surely sounds like one for whom the relation between Christ and culture is paradoxical.

Or consider Luther. We might expect him, as a dualist, to believe that sometimes, in order to sustain our community's way of life, we may need to do boldly the evil that Christ seems to forbid. But in his treatise *On Temporal Authority*, considering what St. Paul calls government's "power of the sword," Luther is far from thinking the use of force is an evil that must nevertheless be done. On the contrary, he writes: "Be not so wicked, my friend, as to say, A Christian may not do that which is God's peculiar work, ordinance and creation. . . . If it is God's work and creation, it is good, and so good that every one can use it in a Christian and saving way." That does not sound much like one who lives with a constant sense of paradoxical tension.

In short, we cannot expect the typology, insightful as it is, to do our thinking for us or answer the questions we confront. What it can do, however, is help us think more clearly and carefully about ways in which the lives of Christian people are often drawn in two directions—and thereby help us come to terms with both the spirit and the structure of Christian life.

PART II

The Spirit of the Christian Life

SEVEN

Christian Love

Having canvassed the gifts bestowed on the church by Christ's Spirit, St. Paul concludes the thirteenth chapter of I Corinthians with the well-known words: "So faith, hope, love abide, these three; but the greatest of these is love." If by "abide" we mean "abide eternally in the new creation God promises," then "abide" is probably not the best translation. After all, it makes little sense to say that hope will abide in that new creation. More likely St. Paul means that of all the spiritual gifts he has discussed, there remain three that are central—faith, hope, and love.

This is not the only time Paul highlights these three virtues of the Christian life. His greeting to the Colossians (1:3–5) gives thanks for the faith they have as people who live in Christ Jesus, for the love they show to fellow believers, and for the hope for God's promised future that undergirds their faith and love. Writing to the Thessalonian church he greets them in similar fashion—thanking God for their faith, their works of love, and their steadfast hope in Jesus (I Thess. 1:3). Thus, we see in Paul's letters the centrality of what came in Christian tradition to be called the theological virtues.

Nevertheless, the greatest of these, as St. Paul is at pains to underscore, is the love for which Christians have regularly used the Greek word that Paul himself used, *agape* (translated into Latin as *caritas*, from which the English word "charity" is derived). Jesus summarizes the moral law in terms of the twofold command to love God and the neighbor (Mark 12:28–31). St. Paul's statement, "he who loves his neighbor has fulfilled the law" (Rom. 13:8) is more compressed still. St. Augustine (in *On the Morals of the Catholic Church*) defines the cardinal virtues (temperance, fortitude, justice, and prudence) as forms of love. Nevertheless, there is no single, entirely satisfactory way to define agape as Christians have understood it.

It is no surprise, therefore, that, when characterizing love, Christians have often resorted to stories or illustrations—for example, the parable of Jesus (recounted in Luke 15) that is often called the Prodigal Son. Actually, of course, it is less a story about the son than about a father and his two sons. Reading or hearing the story, we may be moved to characterize love in various ways. The father's love for the prodigal seems to demand nothing in return. It is self-giving, even to the point of self-sacrifice—as, for example, when the father loses his dignity running to welcome his returning son, or when we suspect that he may suffer still more from the behavior of the older son. In addition to being so heedless of self, his is a love that does not seem to depend upon any qualifications in the loved one; for the father brushes aside the returning prodigal's attempts to qualify for renewed acceptance.

Just as striking and well known is the parable of the Good Samaritan (in Luke 10). Given the cultural and religious divides of that time and place, we might not expect that the Samaritan would stop to help the man who was beaten and now lies by the roadside.

The victimized man has no special claim on the Samaritan and is in no position to return any help the Samaritan may provide. The Samaritan simply honors the being of the victim and cares for his well-being. Using his own resources of time and wealth to provide for the beaten man, he demonstrates, as did the prodigal's father, a kind of self-giving that borders on self-sacrifice.

Such stories teach us to describe agape in different ways, appreciating its richness. It is selfless, as were the Samaritan and the Prodigal's father. It requires nothing in return for the care it offers. It is non-comparative, caring both for those who seem deserving and for those who clearly are not. It simply affirms the being and the well-being of others. We can see a love something like this enacted in a charming little poem written by the six-year-old daughter of the philosopher J. L. Stocks (in his book *Morality and Purpose*)—a poem written to her bicycle:

> O beautiful bike, I love you so:
> It is so nice to see you go.
> I will wash you and clean you and take you home—
> O beautiful bike, will you come?

Her love for the bike may begin with a certain possessiveness—desiring to take it home with her. But that eagerness to possess is transformed into an appreciative love. To use the language of everyday life, we could borrow from Josef Pieper and think of her as saying to the bike, "It's good that you exist." Good whether or not you come home with me and are mine. Good simply that you should be.

Self-love

Jesus gives his followers what he calls a "new command," one that in some ways goes beyond even the dual command to love God and the neighbor. That new command is that they should love one another "as I have loved you" (John 13:34). If Jesus' own self-sacrificing love is to be the pattern for ours, the stakes have been raised considerably. In particular, we must surely wonder whether any concern for oneself, any self-love, can meet the standard of this new command given by one who willingly goes to the cross. And yet, a world in which we expend ourselves entirely in service of others, heedless of our own needs or desires, may come to seem self-destructive.

Is there such a thing as proper self-love? I am not sure there is a theoretically adequate answer to that question. Those who have read and discussed with others Shel Silverstein's children's book, *The Giving Tree,* will know firsthand how complicated the question is. Readers are even likely to disagree about whether *The Giving Tree* is a book that should be read to children. Throughout the story, and through all the stages of his life, the boy keeps returning to the Tree, seeking its help to meet his needs. He needs money, a house, a chance to get away. And each time he comes back, the Tree gives—first her apples and leaves, and, in the end, her very substance (her branches and trunk). When the boy returns one last time, it is to a Tree that is now merely a stump. "And the Tree was happy." Or so we read. But not all readers will agree. Indeed, almost any group of readers is likely to engage in spirited disagreement about the book and its message. I am not at all certain we can find a theory of Christian love that makes neither too much nor too little of self-love.

In his influential book, *Agape*, Gene Outka delineated four different ways Christian thinkers have assessed self-love. For some it is considered "wholly nefarious" and is forbidden for Christians. Others have held that self-love is "normal, reasonable, and prudent." Hence, while it may sometimes lapse into selfishness, it may just as often be an ordinary feature of life that provides a standard for how we should love others. A third Christian perspective justifies self-love "derivatively." That is, in order to care appropriately for others and not unduly to burden them, and sometimes in order to make clear to others how they must treat their fellow human beings, we may need to look to our own interests and needs. And finally, some might argue that, if agape requires that we will to exist equally for every human being, we must include not just others but also ourselves within the scope of that equal regard.

If we think of agape simply as an ethical principle divorced from any setting within Christian theology, there might be much to be said for the fourth assessment of self-love. In principle, after all, it may be hard to show why we should not love the self as much (if no more than) others. But, of course, if there are Christian reasons to draw back from that approach, we may conclude that agape cannot adequately be characterized as an ethical principle if abstracted from a connection with other Christian beliefs. To believe that we have been incorporated into the risen Christ is to believe that we are ultimately secure, that we need have no ultimate concern for our own well-being, since God has seen to it. Of course, this does not mean that we abandon our own projects in the world, as if acceptance by God meant loss of self. But it may mean that the focus of our concern has been decisively shifted—from a love that counts our needs as equal to that of all others to a love that focuses chiefly on the needs of neighbors.

Hence, to say that self-love should not be at the center of our lives as Christians is not to say that we should go through life without our own interests, plans, and projects. Indeed, we could make no sense of a love focused on serving neighbors' needs if they had no interests, desires, or projects of their own. Hence, to say, as that first approach to self-love does, that it is forbidden for

Christians must mean simply that commitment to the well-being of others will sometimes have to keep us from fulfilling some of our own desires. It need not—indeed, ought not—be taken to deny that God calls each of us to particular tasks in life—that each person's pilgrimage toward God will follow its own distinctive course. Some will be more obviously self-denying than others. The life course another person takes may be good for him, his calling, but not for me. We go wrong only if we live in a way that never seems to ask of us any self-denial. More than that, however, we probably should not claim.

There is an instructive illustration of this in Charlotte Brontë's great novel, *Jane Eyre*. Fairly late in the novel, but before Jane is reunited with Mr. Rochester, she comes to know two sisters (Diana and Mary) and their brother, the minister St. John Rivers. He is in many ways a tormented soul. Jane notices that he does not seem "to enjoy that mental serenity, that inward content," that she would have expected to find in him. Instead, he feels called—driven—to go as a missionary to India, sacrificing other desires (including the desire for marriage) in order to expend himself utterly in that work. And he wants Jane to accompany him there, not as a wife but as a helper, sacrificing for the sake of the work her need for love and emotional support. Describing to Jane St. John's sense of calling, his sister, Diana, characterizes him as "inexorable as death." Yet, she says, "I cannot for a moment blame him for it. It is right, noble, Christian; yet it breaks my heart." In the end, Jane decides that she cannot accompany St. John to India.

It is, however, both striking and thought-provoking that, even after Jane has been reunited—by what must seem to be the hand of Providence—with Mr. Rochester and has married him, the final three paragraphs of the novel are devoted to bringing readers up to date on St. John and his ongoing work. "He entered on the path he had marked for himself; he pursues it still." And in the end he will be among those "who are called, chosen, and faithful." In a thoughtful essay on *Jane Eyre*, Professor Jerome Beaty notes that modern readers have often found something harsh and "anti-life" in St. John's chosen course. But the truth, Beaty suggests, is simply that "his way is not Jane's way." His pilgrimage through life may call for self-denial and sacrifice of ordinary pleasures; hers takes its course "through everyday, domestic life." Jane's way of life would be wrong for St. John; his would be wrong for her. "Her way and her life story, her narrating 'I,' are decentered, not just to make room for St. John but to reveal the real center, which, in the world of Brontë's novel, is always and everywhere God"—the God who calls each of them, each of us, to love in particular ways.[18]

Reciprocity in Love

Even if in this way we give a kind of qualified approval to self-love—or, at least, acknowledge the truth that commitment to our own plans and projects, our own course of life, is permissible and appropriate—we still need to consider another, related but slightly different, question about the nature of agape. Should we expect, or even require, that the love we show to others be reciprocated?

This question exists—as an unresolved one—within the Gospels themselves. In the Gospel of John (15:12) Jesus commands his disciples to "love one another as I have loved you." Earlier we noted how this command, establishing Jesus' self-sacrificing love as the standard for his followers, forces us to wonder whether self-love can have any place within the Christian life. Now, though, we must also note that it seems to make mutuality and reciprocity central in agape. It suggests a warmth and intimacy that are not really present in Jesus' well-known words in the Sermon on the Mount: "If you love those who love you, what reward have you? . . . And if you salute only your brethren, what more are you doing than others?" (Mt. 5:46ff.)

And, in fact, we can understand why, for some people, a love that seems not even to worry whether it is returned might lack the warmth and intimacy that (we suppose) Christian love ought to have. Scholars have often argued as much. So, for example, Margaret Farley contends (in *Personal Commitments*) that genuine love must involve an affective union. More important still, to eliminate any element of reciprocity from the life of love threatens to miss a crucial aspect of our creaturely life—namely, our neediness. A self-sufficiency that needs no return of its love may, in fact, be closer to the "ruthless, sleepless, unsmiling concentration upon self" that C. S. Lewis, in his Preface to *The Screwtape Letters*, called "the mark of Hell."

Perhaps, in fact, a certain kind of neediness and reciprocity also characterizes the Creator. For the inner life of the Triune God is itself always marked not only by giving but also by receiving. "Even within the Holy One Himself," C. S. Lewis once wrote, "it is not sufficient that the Word should *be* God, it must also be *with* God." And in this way "the union of reciprocal loves" that constitutes the Triune God "may transcend mere arithmetical unity or self-identity."[19] Thus, from eternity the Father gives all that he is and has to the Son; from eternity the Son offers that begotten life back to his Father; and from eternity the Spirit is the bond of their mutual love, presenting (as Robert Jenson put it) the Son to the Father as the object of his love and the Father to the Son as the one who loves him. "God is what happens between Jesus and his Father in their Spirit."[20] That is to say, the one God is an event, a happening in which love is constantly given and returned. And in coming into our lives through the Spirit of Christ, that one God makes room for us—opens up space for us within the giving and receiving that never stops within the divine life. In such self-giving love, but reciprocated self-giving, "we touch," as Lewis put it, "a rhythm not only of all creation but of all being."[21]

Robert Jenson once suggested that this one God who is Father, Son, and Spirit is a little bit like the sort of complex musical composition that is called a fugue.[22] In a fugue a theme is first introduced in one voice. Then that theme is taken up by another voice, and yet another, as they interweave constantly throughout. Learning to hear that interweaving can be hard—quite hard, perhaps, for some of us.

There is a nice illustration of this very near the end of *Gaudy Night*, one of Dorothy Sayers' Lord Peter Wimsey mysteries. Harriet Vane and Lord Peter are attending a concert in which Bach's Concerto in D Minor for two violins is being played. Lord Peter, it says, "was wrapt in the motionless austerity with which all genuine musicians listen to genuine music." Unlike Harriet, who knew just enough "to read the sounds a little with her brains, laboriously unwinding the twined chains of melody link by link," Peter "could hear the whole intricate pattern, every part separately and simultaneously, each independent and equal, separate but inseparable, moving over and under and through, ravishing heart and mind together."

The Triune God is a little like that sort of melody—each voice independent and equal, separate but inseparable, moving over and under and through. And when such a God one day completes the work of making space for us within his own life, the love that here and now continually calls us out of ourselves and sometimes goes unanswered will receive its proper return. Short of that day, however, we must, as Koheleth says, cast our bread upon the waters. Love is not love if it gives only in hope of a return. But love is not love unless it also hopes to share in a union of reciprocal loves.

EIGHT

Preference in Love

In Jane Austen's novel *Emma*, a man named Mr. Weston has married the woman who had been Emma's governess and also her close friend and confidant. Emma, whose judgment is not always the best, has mixed feelings about Mr. Weston. He seems to be on good terms and friendly with everyone he meets, and Emma admires his "open manners." But she also has reservations about this openness of his character. He seems just a little too amiable and friendly with all his acquaintances. And in Emma's mind "general benevolence, but not general friendship, made a man what he ought to be."

Emma's character faults notwithstanding, she has a point. If a man is a friend to everyone who comes along, we might wonder whether he is really a friend to anyone. Friendly perhaps, but not a friend. It would be strange to suppose that we did not care about our friends for particular reasons, that we did not prefer them to others for just those reasons. Yet, of course, one might argue that Mr. Weston's character, as Emma describes it, is rather like Jesus' depiction (in Mt. 5:45) of the heavenly Father, who "makes his sun rise on the evil and on the good, and sends rain on the just and on the unjust."

In the previous chapter's discussion of the nature of agape—exploring the place, if any within agape, of self-love and a desire that one's love be reciprocated—we considered the depiction of love in Jesus' parable of the Good Samaritan. The Samaritan's love seems almost entirely selfless, simply caring for the victimized man, affirming both his being and his well-being. The compressed story told in the parable is powerful, and that no doubt helps to explain why it is among the most well-known of biblical stories. But it is powerful, at least in part, because it is so compressed. One man, lying beaten by the side of the road; another man passing by, faced with a decision whether to help. Suppose we complicate Jesus' parable a little (in a way first suggested to me years ago by Bruce Hucker).

Suppose that a contemporary would-be Good Samaritan, passing by, were to see not one but three men lying beaten by the side of the road. All are bleeding profusely, all seem to be equally in need of immediate attention and care, but the Samaritan must help one while, in all likelihood, the others die before they too can be helped. When he looks at the three victims, the Samaritan, to his surprise, realizes that he recognizes each of them. The first he does not know personally, but he recognizes him as a medical researcher reputed to be on the verge of important breakthroughs. The second he knows very well; for this victim has been a critic and enemy of the Samaritan for years. And the third is the Samaritan's son. What now? The story is still powerful, but it no longer seems clear or obvious. Even if the Samaritan wants to be a neighbor to each of the three, the limits of time and place make it impossible for him to treat them identically.

If all three were complete strangers to him, the Samaritan could hardly do better than flip a coin—or, in this case, perhaps simply help the one nearest to him. But these three are not strangers to him, and each might have a different sort of claim on him for care. Saving the medical researcher is likely to produce the greatest long-term benefits, not only for the researcher himself but also for many others who may benefit from his continued work. But, of course, beneficial consequences are by no means the only—or, even necessarily, the most important—moral consideration. To give them priority here might be more like adhering to a principle than actually loving a neighbor.

What about the enemy? Is there a case to be made for attending to his injuries? Well, of course, there is, at least if we aim to take seriously Jesus' teaching in the Sermon on the Mount: "You have heard that it was said, 'You shall love your neighbor and hate your enemy.' But I say to you, Love your enemies and pray for those who persecute you.'" That would settle the matter, were the Samaritan's enemy the only injured victim. But in this instance he is not, and there is no reason to think that his claim for care is stronger than that of the others. One might say—Kierkegaard says something like this when recommending works of love for the dead—that caring for those who cannot or will not reciprocate our love ensures that our love is pure. But surely, that cannot be the point, for in saying this he subtly shifts the focus from the neighbor in need to himself.

Faced with this choice, most of us would surely try to save the life of our son. Not to focus first on him would seem to ignore the creaturely bonds God uses to sustain and enrich human life. Even granting this, however, we might still be worried that we had allowed preference such a central place in our behavior. We need, therefore, to think through that choice by examining more systematically the possible ways to justify such preference within a life of agape. There are roughly three different ways that Christian thinkers have tried to make place within the Christian life for such preference without denying that we are called to be a neighbor to every human being.

A first approach is to build *around* our other loves with the non-preferential agape love. From this perspective we begin with the recognition that there are other loves in addition to agape; we do not seek a unified concept of love. Many of our loves are grounded in particular relations that give us reason to show special preference to and care for certain people—family members, friends, fellow-citizens—rather than to others. This is not contrary to the will of God, who, as St. Paul said to the men of Athens, determines the places and allots the times to different peoples (Acts 17:26). So this first approach begins by acknowledging that much of a Christian's life does not have its roots in agape. There are other loves, other special relationships, to which God calls us, and there is nothing wrong with that. Nevertheless, recognizing that such special preference can sometimes lead us to wrong others who are not so closely connected to us, the equal neighbor-love enjoined by agape must build around those preferential loves, fencing them in and keeping preference within bounds.

There is much to be said for this approach; indeed, it has a commonsense quality that is likely to appeal to many of us. It gives agape an important role to play in the Christian life without attempting to make it the whole of that life. Agape sets limits, specifying what we ought never do to any neighbor. As long as we remain within those boundaries as best we can, doing no injury or injustice to others, we are left free to pursue our special, preferential loves and attachments. For all its appeal, however, this way of understanding agape may not seem entirely satisfactory. It makes the love that is central in Christian life seem rather pale and anemic—a purely negative principle, setting boundaries in life, but doing little else. It seems to miss the positive, active character of Christian love, and in that way may fail to capture the energy and power that agape should bring.

We might, therefore, consider other possibilities. There are two other approaches that give greater centrality to agape by seeking a more unified concept of love, making our other loves less independent and drawing them into closer relation with equal neighbor-love.

A second approach could begin with agape's equal neighbor-love and build *down* from it, incorporating into it our other, particular and preferential, loves. With that staring point, agape would be more central, more than a negative principle that builds a protective fence around other loves. The agape that the Good Samaritan seems to embody would now clearly have first place in the Christian life. What then of other loves? What place could they have?

If building around our other loves might threaten to make too little of agape, to deprive it of centrality, this second approach may make it hard to find a place within the Christian life for other loves. Clearly, because we are limited, finite beings, there must always be limits to the scope of our love. Inevitably, it seems, we will love some more than others. Yet, beginning with agape love that wills to exist equally for every human being, how are we to justify showing special consideration to those who are closely connected to us? We can, of course, pray for all people and wish them well, but our time and energy will necessarily be devoted to a smaller circle of family, friends, and acquaintances. How to justify that? When we begin with agape and build down, we seek to incorporate other loves into life as specifications—particular instances or applications—of our more general benevolence toward all.

Appealing as this approach is, does it really work? To be sure, it is true that, because we are finite, the scope of our love will be limited. But why should it be limited to those with whom we have special ties, those whom we prefer? We do not love our friends and family members simply because we must love some and they are near at hand. We do not think of them simply as specific examples of a love we have for all people. On the contrary, those particular and preferential loves have an urgency about them that makes them something other than an instance of general benevolence toward all.

That leaves a third approach, another attempt at a unified understanding of agape and other loves. Rather than attempting to derive particular loves from agape—which, as we have seen, is not easy to do—we may begin with our preferential attachments and build *up* from them to a more universal neighbor-love. Our particular loves become a kind of training ground in which we slowly become persons who are better able to love. As St. Augustine says in his *City of God* (1.29), believers "have no reason to regret even this life of time, for in it they are schooled for eternity." That is to say, committing ourselves to those we love, even when those loves are partial and preferential, means entering into a school of virtue in which and through which our loves are broadened and purified.

Learning what a transformation of our character is required to learn to love just a few who have been given to us in special relations, we may gradually become people more able to love even those to whom we have no special attachment, even those lying beaten by the side of the road. In this way our love may gradually become something more like genuine agape. To be sure, this process of training is likely to take the whole of one's life and can come to full fruition only in the new creation that is promised. But this simply means that love must be accompanied by faith and hope.

Building up from particular loves to agape is an approach that was perhaps first articulated by St. Augustine. We can give the final word on the place of preference within Christian love to what Augustine says in Book I of his work *On Christian Doctrine*. All are to be loved equally, he writes,

> but since you cannot be of assistance to everyone, those especially are to be cared for who are most closely bound to you by place, time, or opportunity, as if by chance. Thus suppose you had an abundance of something which it would be well to give to someone else who lacked it, but you could not give it to two. If two came to you of whom neither took precedence either in need or in any special connection with you, you could do nothing more just than to decide by lot which one should be given that which you could not give to both. Thus in the same way among men, not all of whom you can care for, you must consider as if selected by lot each one as he is able to be more closely associated with you in time.

Hence, that would-be Good Samaritan forced to choose one of the three to help could with a good conscience bind up the wounds of his son. All three victims are bound to him by "opportunity," but the son is bound also by "place" and "time." The Creator has cast lots among them, setting the solitary in families and thereby giving preference to the son. But that cannot be the end of the story; for that would-be Good Samaritan must begin to become a person who, as much as he is able, will seek to care for all even as he cares for his son. Only in that way can preference find an acceptable place within the life of agape.

NINE

Love and God's Commands

In the novel *Jane Eyre*, there comes a moment when Jane must make an excruciating decision. She and Mr. Rochester had been on the very brink of exchanging marriage vows when the secret of his marriage years ago—to a woman who, though insane, was still living—had been revealed. He pleads with Jane to ignore that ill-fated marriage and live with him as his wife. Both Jane's reason and feeling, every fiber of her being, move her to comply. Who could possibly be injured if she were to agree? But in fact, she realizes, she would be injured if she were not to "keep the law given by God; sanctioned by man."

> Laws and principles are not for the times when there is no temptation. They are for such moments as this, when body and soul rise in mutiny against their rigour. . . . If at my individual convenience I might break them, what would be their worth? They have a worth—so I have

> always believed; and if I cannot believe it now, it is because I am insane—quite insane: with my veins running fire, and my heart beating faster than I can count its throbs. Preconceived opinions, foregone determinations, are all I have at this hour to stand by: there I plant my foot.[23]

To be sure, someone reading this might call Jane a "legalist," but that would be to miss the point rather badly, would it not?

Christian thinkers have sometimes characterized as legalists those who think that some moral questions can, so to speak, be judged in advance, because the action either conforms to God's commands or does not. Helmut Thielicke expressed a view held by many when he wrote that such a view would not let a person be "the acting subject in the making of his own decision." Surely, however, that cannot be the right way to characterize Jane's insistence that she will not comply with Mr. Rochester's wishes. It is precisely her commitment to keep the moral law that empowers Jane and enables her to find wholeness and agency within herself even when both reason and feeling move her to do otherwise. And we readers may well admire her for this.

The Calling and Its Limits

Evidently there is a little more to be said for moral rules than some Christians have sometimes thought. Jane's adherence to God's commands does not seem to undermine either her agency or the freedom with which she acts. In fact, in a passage that Jane might have welcomed, Dietrich Bonhoeffer once suggested (in his little book on the psalms) that it is "grace to know God's commands. They free us from self-made plans and conflicts. They make our steps certain and our way joyful." It is only when we separate the moral life from the life of faith that we miss the grace of which Bonhoeffer writes. Separating life from faith may indeed make legalists of us—as if our moral judgments were not enclosed within a life transformed by Christ. Or, alternatively, that separation may turn us into what the tradition has called antinomians—people who suppose that being in Christ does not provide a form or shape to our behavior.

To be sure, when as Christians we keep God's commands as best we can, we are not simply adhering to a rule. We are finding the vocation to which God calls us day after day, new each day. Planting our foot in such obedience, as Jane did, is neither an achievement of ours nor a possession on which we can simply depend. Rather, it is part of our life in Christ, a life of faith in the God whose command is our calling. This is the way St. Paul described his own life—"under the law of Christ" (I Cor. 9:21)—even as he urged the Galatians to "fulfill the law of Christ" (Gal. 6:2). It is the way of life of all who, as the psalmist says, "delight in the law of the Lord" (Ps. 1:2).

It is worth our reflecting again on what Jane realizes in that decisive moment—namely, that our actions do more than bring about results in the world. Our actions also express the person we are and help to shape the person we will become. They indicate whether we are people who will trust God to care for us and for the world, or whether we think we must shoulder that burden ourselves. For God calls us to faithfulness in the tasks we are given—no less than that, but also no more. C. S. Lewis once observed that we should think of ourselves as characters in a play that is written and directed by the divine dramatist.

> We do not know the play. We do not even know whether we are in Act I or Act V. We do not know who are the major and who the minor characters. The Author knows. . . .

> That it has a meaning we may be sure, but we cannot see it. When it is over, we may be told. We are led to expect that the Author will have something to say to each of us on the part that each of us has played. The playing it well is what matters infinitely.[24]

Hence, to listen for the command and call of God is, perhaps strangely to our minds, to be set free. Free, that is, to discern the limits that should govern and guide even our attempts to accomplish what is both needed and good. This means, of course and unfortunately, that there may be worthy goals we would like to achieve but can find no permissible way to pursue. There may be suffering we might relieve but ought not—ought not because we can find no way to do so that is in keeping with our life in Christ. This does not mean that we ignore a neighbor's need simply in order to adhere to a rule or keep our hands clean. It means that we must love according to the reality of what is loved. It means that to sin for the sake of a neighbor is to make of that person more than he or she truly is—namely, a *creature*, who must always be loved in relation to God.

Of course, Christians may sometimes find good reason to change their approach to a moral question. Perhaps the most important instance of this in the history of the church is that recounted by Luke in chapters 10 and 11 of *The Acts of the Apostles*. Cornelius, a Gentile centurion in Caesarea, is told in a vision to send his servants to find Peter in Joppa and ask him to come and speak with Cornelius and his household. At the same time, Peter himself in a vision has been invited to kill and eat animals, reptiles, and birds—many of them forbidden for Jews to eat. Hesitating to eat what has been forbidden, Peter hears a voice that says, "What God has cleansed, you must not call common."

Unsure what all this may mean, Peter goes with the servants to the home of Cornelius in Caesarea. Invited to speak, he tells them the "good news of peace by Jesus Christ," good news that reaches its climax when God raises Jesus on the third day. And while Peter was recounting all this, Luke writes, "the Holy Spirit fell on all who heard the word. And the believers from among the circumcised who came with Peter were amazed, because the gift of the Holy Spirit had been poured out even on the Gentiles"—Gentiles whom Peter then baptizes.

This was by no means the end of the story, however. We could sooner say it was the beginning—the beginning of conversations between Peter and the leaders in Jerusalem of the fledgling movement of Jesus' followers. Peter reports his vision and what he has done, and Luke's summary conclusion is that the Jerusalem leaders realized that God had granted "repentance unto life" also to Gentiles. We know, however, that the story is much longer. We know, for instance, that the mission of St. Paul to Gentiles raised similar complicated questions for those early Christians, as the story in Acts 15 of the Jerusalem conference indicates. It is clear that these first Christians did not simply change their mind on the basis of Peter's (or Paul's) experience. On the contrary, that experience led them to search the Scriptures, exploring in more detail the way the Lord's work in Israel's history had been moving toward a day when Gentiles would be grafted onto the vine that was Israel. Richard Hays makes the point nicely:

> The church did not simply observe the experience of Cornelius and his household and decide that Scripture must be wrong after all. On the contrary, the experience of uncircumcised Gentiles responding in faith to the gospel message led the church back to a new reading of

> Scripture. . . . Only because the new experience of Gentile converts proved *hermeneutically illuminating* of Scripture, was the church, over time, able to accept the decision to embrace Gentiles within the fellowship of God's people.[25]

Recalling C. S. Lewis's suggestion that we think of ourselves as characters in a play whose author is God should remind us that we are not likely to discern God's call to us if we listen for it in isolation. On the contrary, the development of the moral life is seldom a solo endeavor, for it is as the Body of Christ that Christians read—and read again—the Scriptures of Israel and of the evangelists and apostles, seeking to hear the command of God.

Compromise

To hear God's commands and strive to live in accord with them is, as I noted above, not simply adhering to a rule. It is listening for the call of God, for our vocation. That may, however, be too simple a way of putting it, for there is also a sense in which morality and vocation are not simply identical. When we are graced, as Bonhoeffer says, to know God's commands, what we know is the moral order built into the creation, distorted by our sin, but vindicated in the resurrection of Jesus. That moral order is one thing; God's call to me as a particular person is another. So, for example, although the goodness of marriage is written into the creation, God may call any of us to the celibate life.

For reasons perhaps somewhat autobiographical in character, Kierkegaard was especially struck by a possible tension between the moral order and particular vocations—a tension powerfully depicted in *Fear and Trembling*. The moral order written into the creation forbids one person to murder another. Yet, Abraham is called by

God to sacrifice his son, Isaac. Kierkegaard describes Abraham's obedience to this calling as a "teleological suspension of the ethical." That is, in order to live in personal relationship with God and respond to his calling, in order to make that the goal and purpose of his life, Abraham must suspend the ordinary moral requirement.

We know, of course, that the story ends with Abraham being delivered from that choice. The ethical that he has teleologically suspended is returned to him. Nonetheless, Kierkegaard is not wrong to remind us that life in Christ is more than obedience to the commands by which God structures all our lives. It is also free response to his call.

It is, therefore, hard to know what to say about the fact that sometimes moral compromise that falls short of what God commands may seem to be our only possibility. This is not really surprising, for the moral order embedded by God in creation has been *dis*ordered by sin. We cannot escape that disorder while living in this world. Thus, St. Paul wrote to the Corinthians (5:9–10): "I wrote to you in my letter not to associate with immoral men; not at all meaning the immoral of this world, or the greedy and robbers, or idolaters, since then you would need to go out of the world." We do not and cannot always know with any clarity the difficulties and struggles that mark others' lives and turn them in the direction of moral compromise; for there is, after all, an inevitable element of privacy in the conditions others face. Hence, we may not easily know what we can ask of them. And, of course, not only others but also we ourselves may at times have to act in circumstances where every course of action open to us, insofar as we can discern its complications, seems to undermine our moral commitments.

This does not mean, as Helmut Thielicke put it, that "we live in a perpetual night in which all cats are gray." But it reminds us all too powerfully that God's good creation is so disordered by sin that human reason and insight may sometimes find no way to penetrate through the darkness into the light. It is, however, all too easy to turn this fact about our sinful world into a belief that the only thing that matters is our inner faith in God's acceptance—and that such faith is compatible with actions which we know contradict the lordship of Christ. For that reason, Thielicke, who had many occasions to think through the problem of moral compromise during the years of Nazi rule in Germany, felt compelled to remind his readers that we may not "get off the hook of God's unconditional requirement" by observing that the world is evil and distorted by sin. For, as he observes, that world is our doing and "the objectification" of the human ego. Therefore, "any simple affirmation of compromise" is not permitted us. We must, he writes, "leave the requirement of God intact and . . . live provisionally under forgiveness," praying that we may do what is right and that God's will is done through us.

TEN

Marriage as Embodied Love

The bond of marriage between a man and a woman has been very near the center of Christian thinking about the moral life. Indeed, it would be difficult to get closer to that center than does Ephesians 5 in its understanding of the relation between husband and wife as a mysterious image of the bond between Christ and the church. Nevertheless, ours is a world in which marriage has come under enormous strain and been redefined in various ways. And perhaps the most helpful way to think about marriage as Christians traditionally understood it is to consider the difference between that traditional view and a more recent, revisionist understanding. Only in this way, I think, can we appreciate what gives the traditional view its theological coherence.

We can approach these two contrasting views indirectly, though, by considering a passage from the book, *Choosing a Sex*

Ethic, by the Jewish rabbi and philosopher, Eugene Borowitz. He invites us to consider

> a choice between two possible situations. Neither is really satisfactory, yet they represent what life offers to many people. In one case, we will find love, rich and moving, but never great enough to result in marriage. Thus, while such affairs last months or even years, each inevitably ends, and the lovers go their separate ways. The other possibility is of a life spent in a marriage but not one initiated because of love. The couple has very genuine regard for one another, but it cannot be said to rise to that level of empathy and passion we call love. Yet knowing themselves to be unlikely to have a much richer emotional experience or to have a better partner with whom to spend their lives, they marry. Would you prefer a life of love that never comes to marriage over a life of marriage that knows regard but not love?[26]

To be sure, Borowitz understands that we want both and perhaps can have both, but he still thinks the thought experiment is instructive. And he is clear about which he himself would choose. "Seen from the perspective of time and a whole life, if there must be a choice, then being married, even only in deep friendship, seems to me far more personally significant than being in love from time to time. . . . I value ecstasy, but I believe in almost every case becoming a person is more truly bound up with perseverance."

We should not, I think, be surprised that a Jewish believer would make such a choice. For Jews, together with Christians, share a tradition in which the body has profound importance for the meaning of our humanity. Human beings were created in bodily form (from the dust of the ground), and—as Christians in particular emphasize—we will one day be raised to a life that, though transformed, does not leave the body behind. Indeed, it is this belief about the end-time resurrection of the body that enables the church fully to affirm the body. Thus, St. Paul emphasizes to the Corinthian church (in I Corinthians 15) that hope for the resurrection of the body is central to what Christians believe and teach. Understandably, therefore, many of the problems that troubled the Corinthian church—in particular, sexual immorality and rejection of sexual relations within marriage—testified to a belief that our embodied nature was of little moral consequence. When, by contrast, we emphasize that human life is an embodied life, it will be clear that such life requires—as Borowitz emphasized—a history over time, a history of covenant commitments that is not just a series of isolated moments.

To think through the meaning of embodied life more fully, we can sketch out—in admittedly schematic fashion—two contrasting views, traditional and revisionist, of marriage.

Traditional

What is the significance of saying that God creates human beings as a sexually differentiated species, as male and female? It does not mean that God creates a subjective consciousness and then adds to it a male or female body. Rather, it means that God creates beings who are marked by the sexual differentiation, by their bodies. The body is not something the person uses; the person is present in the body, in its actions and passions. Hence, we know persons only as we encounter them as male or female. We can explore what that means in relation to four different aspects of the marriage bond.

Consider first the meaning of the presence of *children* for marriage. In the traditional Christian view, which considers our embodied condition to have moral significance, the marital union of a man and a woman should ordinarily hope to be fruitful. After all, their sexual union is ordered toward offspring. We can even say that they should not marry unless they are at least willing to have that happen. There are, of course, intramural Christian disagreements about exactly how to interpret this belief that the sexual relationship within marriage should remain open to children. For some—Roman Catholics in particular—the view has been that contraceptive intercourse is wrong and that every marital act should be open to the transmission of life. For other Christians it has seemed better to say that the marriage bond as a whole, over time, should be open to the presence of children.

Still, the general agreement has been that love-giving should also hope to be life-giving. Sexual intercourse between husband and wife is not only intended to bring pleasure and fulfillment to their union. It does that, of course, but to think that is its only point would be to miss the meaning of the bodily relationship. For, in addition, our creation as male and female—as embodied beings of that sort—clearly sets before us a task: to be fruitful and multiply.

A second feature of the traditional view focuses on *permanence*. Christians have traditionally believed that the sexual act is appropriate only between those who are married. This is not simply a matter of meeting a legal requirement; more important is that the spouses have made a public, permanent commitment to each other, asking others to regard them as husband and wife. Indeed, only those who have made such a commitment can really be open to the presence of a child.

Why permanence? Precisely for the reason Borowitz noted. What we do in our bodies engages our person. To give the self bodily is not just to hand over a thing for use; it is to give oneself.

No greater form of personal vulnerability can be imagined than that in which we hand ourselves over bodily to another. This commitment so deeply involves our person that it would be short-sighted to think of it as momentary or temporary. Instead, we need to give that commitment a history—a permanent bond over time. Only such a commitment takes with full seriousness the presence of the person in the giving of the body.

A third feature of the traditional view emphasizes the *sexual differentiation* of the married partners. If by God's creative gift the male-female differentiation is the fundamental form of human community, we are called to honor and uphold that distinction. Created as male *and* female, it follows, as Karl Barth put it, that we should live as male *or* female. Hence, it will not be enough that a genital relationship engender and express affection and love. Important as that is, such a relation should also be heterosexual—that is, it should form a bond with one who is other and different from the self, right down to the most fundamental bodily difference. Otherwise, our love is too much like the forbidden love of self. Thus, honoring and upholding in our sexual life the distinction between male and female is part of what it means to live as embodied beings.

Finally, the traditional view invites us to think critically about the increasingly widespread use of *reproductive technologies*. In accord with God's creation, the bodily act by which children are produced is an act of mutual self-giving love. The life-giving act is also a love-giving act. Hence, we are not just using our bodies as a means to produce something desired. Rather, we are giving ourselves, exercising a personal power, in a way that may give rise to a new human being—one who is not just a thing we have made, but one like us, equal to us in dignity. One that is, who has been begotten, not made.

Hence, it will always be problematic for us to transform procreation into a technical act of manufacture. This is not because all rational control of nature is bad, or all technology bad. It is because—knowing ourselves as embodied persons—we know that there is important human significance in the procreative act. In that act we learn that the child is not a thing we have produced but the fruit of self-giving love.

There in schematic outline we can see some of the most important dimensions of the traditional Christian view of marriage. And seeing it this way, we can perhaps begin to see it as a unified whole. From this angle of vision the body is not just a natural object that we are free to use in various ways to accomplish our purposes—so long, of course, as those purposes seem loving. Rather, we are bodies, the body constitutes our person. And by learning to live in accord with our creation as male and female, we honor and uphold God's creation.

Revisionist

In recent decades a competing view of sexuality and marriage has seemed increasingly appealing and persuasive to some Christians. For this view, the moral meaning of the sexual relationship does not depend on its bodily, biological, or procreative dimensions. After all, that bodily nature of life we share with the other animals. It does not constitute our humanity but can "become" human when drawn into a personal bond that is consciously willed and chosen, and marked by care. If moral significance is not tied to the nature of the bodily relation itself, from where does it come? It comes, according to the revisionist view, from the choices we make and the quality of those choices.

We can see more clearly what this means if we think again of the same four dimensions of sexual relationships.

First, then, how might a revisionist view teach us to think about the meaning of the presence of *children*? Imagine, for example, that a man and a woman have a sexual relationship but have no desire at any time now or in the future to have a child. That could, of course, affect the quality of their love in subtle ways, but we can suppose that it need not. And if it does not, and if quality of relationship is what really counts morally, then the fact that their relationship is not only non-procreative but also anti-procreative would have no bearing on its moral quality. The worth of their sexual union stands or falls with the personal fulfillment they give and receive. Nothing more than that need be said.

Second, once we seriously try to think our way into this revisionist approach, it becomes clear that there is no reason why the partners should be married—in the sense of having made a public, *permanent* commitment to each other. They could, as Borowitz hypothesized, understand their relationship as one that is to continue only so long as they both find it fulfilling and satisfying. Indeed, believing, as is often said, that marriage is the grave of love, they might even think it would be wrong to make commitments intended to bind them to each other at some future time when the quality of their relationship had changed. It would be wrong to demand that we continue in relationships that were once, in Borowitz's words, "rich and moving," but are no longer fulfilling or satisfying.

It should now be obvious what the revisionist view would say about the third dimension, *sexual differentiation*. Why should it be necessary that sexual partners be of opposite sexes? Surely those whose desires are for someone of the same sex have the same need for sexual fulfillment as do heterosexuals. And once we have determined that for this view a sexual relation need not be oriented toward the presence of children, we have largely eliminated the sorts of considerations grounded in our embodied nature. Instead, we will simply say that as long as the sexual relation is freely chosen and communicates the needed quality of care and affection, nothing more is needed or should be required.

Finally, there is the fourth dimension—the use of *reproductive technologies*. For the revisionist view it is choice and quality of relationship that count morally. For such a view there is, in principle, no reason why the reproductive act by which human beings come into existence should not be severed completely from the sexual act by which people express and communicate their love for each other. The important moral question about producing children is not how it's done but, simply, whether it is done freely and in love.

Since for this view the biological dimensions of our sexuality take on moral significance only as we consciously will and choose that they should, there is no reason why we should not take control of the reproductive process in very far-reaching ways. Indeed, one could even argue (as Joseph Fletcher did decades ago) that producing children by means of reproductive technologies would be a more human way of doing it. After all, it would be an exercise of freedom and choice, not just submission to the structure of our bodies.

In Search of a Hopeful Word

One final comment about these contrasting visions may be useful here. We should not suppose that we can think about any one of these issues in isolation from the others. We can see this if we consider the tendency within many churches to consider the morality of new reproductive technologies or same-sex relationships as isolated questions that can be considered independently of a more general vision of human sexual love.

Such an approach is unlikely to succeed, for each of these issues is simply a dimension of our sexuality, part of a larger complex of ideas about the moral significance of the fact that human beings are embodied. So, for example, if we think same-sex genital relations are wrong, we should not suppose we can make that argument without also quarreling with the way in which many churches in recent years have made their peace with divorce—as if what matters most is choices we make about desired fulfillment. Patterns of reasoning recur, and we deceive ourselves if we imagine that difficulties we encounter when trying to explain why children are not simply "things" we produce in order to make our life complete are entirely unrelated to ways in which we have compromised the requirement of permanent fidelity in marriage.

These patterns of reasoning are not just about sexuality. They unfold an understanding—different understandings—of what it means to be a human person. Are will and choice at the center of our person? Or are we, first and foremost, animated bodies? Is the human being simply one who chooses and wills—who confers purpose and value by his or her choices? Or is the human being one who also discovers purpose and value in the embodied life God has given us? Is love essentially formless until we give it form? Or is that form imprinted in the structure of our created life?

That, really, is the kind of issue we face today in a world greatly confused about sexual love. The church, therefore, needs to offer the world something more hopeful than the idea that what is good depends simply on our choosing, as if out of our confusions something truly life-affirming could be generated. Instead, the truly hopeful word Christians have to offer—one that gives form to love—is grounded not in our own choices but in God's creation.

ELEVEN

Love and the Loves

The spirit of the Christian life is a love (often called agape love) that simply affirms the being and the well-being of others—saying to them, in Josef Pieper's felicitous formulation, "It's good that you exist." That love does not come naturally to us; it is the gift of Christ's Spirit. But it is also true to say that "love" as we experience it involves much more than this commitment to the well-being of every person. One of the more profound, yet also accessible, explorations of the varieties of love is C. S. Lewis's *The Four Loves*.[27] Although the book is marked in many ways by Lewis's own personal experience, it is also a wise exploration of the relation between agape (or what Lewis calls charity, from the Latin *caritas*) and three other loves that come quite naturally to us: affection, friendship, and eros. For Lewis the relation between these natural loves and charity is complex. Each of the natural loves images in certain ways aspects of charity, and in that sense our understanding of charity presupposes our experience of affection, friendship, and eros. It is also true, however, that charity is needed to perfect those natural loves. Taken alone, they are insufficient and need to become what Lewis calls "modes of charity."

The Power and the Danger of the Natural Loves

The most common instance of affection is the love of family members for each other, although it can also, of course, enter into other loves and shape their character. Affection is, Lewis writes, "the least discriminating of loves." That is, one need not be especially appealing in order to be loved with affection. All that is required is familiarity, a shared common life. "Of all the natural loves it is the most catholic, the least finical, the broadest." And this suggests a sense in which we might say that agape presupposes affection. We gain some insight into what Christian love should be when we see affection at its best, in its healthy state. For, given the requisite familiarity, affection can find something to appreciate in almost anyone. It "opens our eyes to goodness we could not have seen" without it. Thus, it is a little like the God who makes his sun rise on the evil and the good—or like the father who loves both that prodigal son and his elder brother. This gives us one angle, though only one, from which to see what agape is like. For this "least discriminating of loves" offers some sense of what our love must become if we are to say "it's good that you exist" to anyone who crosses our path.

Because our affection is not always healthy, however, agape must also perfect it. Lewis notes a number of respects in which affection can go wrong, and at least two of them seem especially worth our noting. Precisely because affection is so natural a part of life, we may too easily assume that we have a right to be loved—and too easily become jealous and possessive when those by whom we have been loved seem to find new objects of their affection. For affection is, Lewis writes "the most instinctive, in that sense the most animal, of the loves; its jealousy is proportionately fierce." Our affection too readily demands reciprocity and is too easily confused with ownership. When that happens, our affection must be reshaped and perfected by the love that simply says, "It's good that you exist."

Just as we need to be loved with affection, so also we want others to look to us for affection. We need to be needed by them. Deep as the affection of parents for their children usually is, what they may sometimes want for their children is the good that *they* can give, which is not necessarily the good their children genuinely need. To be truly healthy, thc parents' affection "must work toward its own abdication." But that often seems to be more than we can manage. Self-sacrifice we can manage, but self-abdication does not come so easily for affection, even at its best. Therefore, writes Lewis, "a love which desires the good of the object as such, from whatever source that good comes—must step in and help or tame the instinct before it can make the abdication." And therefore, powerful as human affection is, essential for our life as it is, it must be permeated and perfected by the Spirit-given love that is the center of Christian life.

Something similar can be said about the love of friendship. At its best, when healthy, it too shows us something of what agape can be. And it too needs to be reshaped and perfected. Affection is often rooted in a biological tie, grows out of long familiarity, and may seem necessary to everyday life. Friendship, by contrast, is less necessary, more a relation that is freely chosen. "It has no survival value; rather it is one of those things which give value to survival." Hence, we are usually more discriminating in our choice of friends. But if friendship is less discriminating than affection, it is also less jealous—indeed, "the least jealous of loves," Lewis says. Given the limits of time and space, there will, of course, be a limit to the number of people who can share a friendship. But apart from those sorts of physical limits friends are eager to welcome into their circle another who shares the interests that bring them together. They feel no need to keep to themselves those whom they love as friends.

It is not hard to see how our characterization of agape might presuppose some of the qualities we experience in friendship. In its freedom from jealousy, freedom from the need to be needed, and freedom from grounding in biological connection we get helpful images of what Christian love can be. Granting all that, we must also admit, as Lewis does, that friendship can be not only a "school of virtue" but also a "school of vice." Coming together with those who are like-minded and excluding almost by accident those who do not share our interests, we may too easily come to believe that there is something special about our group of friends. Thus, "from the innocent and necessary act of excluding to the spirit of exclusiveness is an easy step; and thence to the degrading pleasure of exclusiveness."

Hence, even at its best friendship is not free of danger. Our friendships can be saved from such danger only as they are perfected by the love that says even to outsiders, "It's good that you exist." We must come to see that our friends are not simply those we have chosen because of their special qualities; they are those God has given us to train us in virtue and make our love genuine. Friendship is the instrument God uses to show us the beauties of a few others, to train us in what it means to love freely. But those beauties "are no greater than the beauties of a thousand" others. And to the degree that our loves are perfected our eyes will be opened to see that beauty in others.

This leaves eros among the natural loves. About eros Lewis makes the same twofold movement. On the one hand, it will image for us divine love; it will give us content to pour into agape. And on the other hand, it too will be inadequate if taken by itself. It too will need to be perfected by becoming a mode of charity.

If ever there was a natural love that gave us an image of what it means to say to another, "It's good that you exist," eros is that love. For what it involves, Lewis writes, is "a delighted pre-occupation with the Beloved." We are familiar with its power to transform us. "In one high bound it has overleaped the massive wall of our selfhood . . . and planted the interests of another in the centre of our being. Spontaneously and without effort we have fulfilled the law (toward one person) by loving our neighbour as ourselves." Thus, eros, when it is healthy, helps to train us in virtue. It can even elicit from us what we otherwise would hardly have dared—a promise of lifelong faithfulness. That commitment is "a paradigm or example, built into our natures, of the love we ought to exercise towards God and Man."

All true, when eros is at its best. But it is not always at its best, and it too needs to be perfected and become a mode of charity. The dangers of eros lie precisely in its great strength and power. When we are possessed by it, "in love," it may seem almost godlike, thinking it can promise lifelong commitment. Its "total commitment" and "transcendence of self-regard" may easily, Lewis suggests, "sound like a message from the eternal world." Yet, eros promises more than, taken by itself, it can deliver. Promising fidelity, it is all too often unfaithful. Experienced as almost godlike, it can easily become an idol, demanding our unconditional allegiance.

Therefore, although it powerfully images for us important aspects of divine love, although we could hardly picture what divine agape is like without the image eros provides, although it is "really and truly like Love Himself," eros too needs to be perfected, transformed into a mode of charity. In that way our love needs to learn faithfulness—not a faithfulness that is within our power, but a faithfulness that is God's gift to us when our loves are drawn into his own love and transformed by it.

The Place of the Natural Loves in the Christian Life

At this point a certain question might naturally occur to us. Once we realize how necessary it is that our natural loves should be perfected and become modes of charity, why not simply turn away from them to agape alone? Why should they play a continuing role in our lives? Why not simply say—equally and identically—to all whom we know, "It's good that you exist"? Lewis underscores in three ways the continuing importance of the natural loves within the Christian life.

First, it should be obvious by now that we need the loves of affection, friendship, and eros as images of divine love. To be sure, each is a partial image even at its best, and each needs to be drawn into divine love in order to be perfected. Nevertheless, without the images they provide, we would have little content to pour into our picture of God's love. Affection's undiscriminating ability to love even those who seem to have little appeal and little to offer, friendship's eagerness to welcome the newcomer, and eros' delighted preoccupation with the loved one—each images for us an aspect of God's love for his creatures.

Second, the natural loves remind us that even God's love cannot be simply a benevolent good will that seeks no return. In their different ways, these natural loves demonstrate that, even if no return is demanded or required, love seeks mutuality as its internal fruition. We could not simply replace the natural loves with a general good will ("it's good that you exist") and still have everything that love is supposed to be.

And third, the natural loves are for us a school of virtue, a necessary preparation in which we begin to be schooled in the meaning of love. They point us to the need for self-abdication, for the close sharing that friendship involves, for loving another as we love ourselves. And in this way they call us out on a long journey that is to culminate in a transformed and perfected love.

At least for here and now, therefore, the Christian life is a journey that incorporates both the natural loves and the divine charity or agape into which those natural loves are being drawn and by which they are being perfected. How to hold them together in our everyday life is not always easy to say. Sometimes, especially when things go well and the natural loves seem relatively healthy, when they seem to image what we suppose divine love must be like, we may think that they are good in themselves and simply need an additional love to complete them. But over time we must surely realize, as Lewis says, that by themselves the natural loves cannot really be themselves unless they become modes of charity. In fact, we may sometimes—even often, perhaps—experience the natural loves and divine charity as almost incompatible rivals in our life. Sufficient experience should teach us, however, that the natural loves cannot, in the end, be satisfactory rivals to charity. For, powerful and important for human life as they are, they cannot stand alone.

Hence, they must become modes of charity, perfected gradually by the love that says to each of us, "It's good that you exist." This transformation is not likely to be painless; for the natural loves, when they are not healthy, may well resist the perfecting they need. Which is to say, we are embarked on a journey in which we are letting ourselves in for something we can scarcely imagine. That is the nature of the life of love God has in mind for us, and Lewis's words are to the point.

We were made for God. Only by being in some respect like Him, only by being a manifestation of His beauty, loving-kindness, wisdom, or goodness, has any earthly Beloved excited our love. It is not that we have loved them too much, but that we did not quite understand what we were loving. It is not that we shall be asked to turn from them, so dearly familiar, to a Stranger. When we see the face of God we shall know that we have always known it.

NOTES

1. C. S. Lewis, *Mere Christianity* (New York: Macmillan, 1960). See chapter 1 ("The Three Parts of Morality") in Book 3: Christian Behaviour.
2. Michael Sandel, "The Case against Perfection," *Atlantic* (April 2004). Available at: https://www.theatlantic.com/magazine/archive/2004/04/the-case-against-perfection/302927/.
3. Alasdair MacIntyre, "Can Medicine Dispense with a Theological Perspective on Human Nature?" pp. 25–43 in *Knowledge, Value and Belief*, ed. H. Tristram Engelhardt and Daniel Callahan (Institute of Society, Ethics and the Life Sciences, 1977).
4. C. S. Lewis, *Perelandra* (New York: Macmillan, 1965), 208.
5. Austin Farrer, *Love Almighty and Ills Unlimited* (Garden City, NY: Doubleday, 1961), 102.
6. Reinhold Niebuhr, *The Nature and Destiny of Man: Volume II. Human Destiny* (New York: Charles Scribner's Sons, 1964), 104.
7. Anders Nygren, *Agape and Eros* (New York and Evanston: Harper & Row, 1969).

8. Mary Grace Mangano, "Christopher Beha left the Catholic church and then came back. Now he's writing a book about why," *America* (March 31, 2022). Available at https://www.americamagazine.org/arts-culture/2022/03/31/christopher-beha-faith-mangano-242710.
9. Roger Angell, "Goodbye Tom," in *Late Innings* (New York: Ballantine Books, 1982), 36.
10. In John N. Wall Jr., ed., *George Herbert: The Country Parson, The Temple* (New York: Paulist Press, 1981), 311.
11. Dietrich Bonhoeffer, *The Cost of Discipleship* (New York: Macmillan, 1963), 277.
12. Michael Wyschogrod, *Abraham's Promise* (Grand Rapids: Eerdmans, 2004), 88.
13. Josef Pieper, *Faith, Hope, Love* (San Francisco: Ignatius Press, 1997), 280–81.
14. Oliver O'Donovan, *The Ways of Judgment* (Grand Rapids: Eerdmans, 2005), 317.
15. H. Richard Niebuhr, *Christ and Culture* (New York: Harper Torchbooks, 1956).
16. Oliver O'Donovan, *The Desire of the Nations* (Cambridge University Press, 1996), 215.
17. Paul Ramsey, "The Transformation of Ethics," in *Faith and Ethics: The Theology of H. Richard Niebuhr*, ed. Paul Ramsey (New York: Harper Torchbooks, 1965). p. 165.
18. Jerome Beaty, "St. John's Way and the Wayward Reader," pp. 491–503 in Charlotte Brontë, *Jane Eyre,* 3rd ed. (New York and London: W. W. Norton, 2001).
19. C. S. Lewis, *The Problem of Pain* (New York: Macmillan, 1962).

20. Robert W. Jenson, *Systematic Theology, Volume 1: The Triune God* (New York and Oxford: Oxford University Press, 1997), 221.
21. Lewis, *The Problem of Pain*, 151–52.
22. Jenson, 235–36.
23. Charlotte Brontë, *Jane Eyre* (New York and London: W. W. Norton, 3rd ed., 2001), 270–71.
24. C. S. Lewis, "The World's Last Night," in Lesley Walmsley (ed.), *C. S. Lewis: Essay Collections and Other Short Pieces* (London: HarperCollins, 2000), 49.
25. Richard B. Hays, *The Moral Vision of the New Testament* (HarperSanFrancisco, 1996), 399.
26. Eugene B. Borowitz, *Choosing a Sex Ethic* (New York: Schocken Books, 1969), 113.
27. C. S. Lewis, *The Four Loves* (New York: Harcourt Brace Jovanovich, 1960).

FURTHER READING

Chapter One

The basic structure and theological underpinnings of this chapter's discussion of approaches to moral reasoning comes, as is evident, from H. Richard Niebuhr's *The Responsible Self.* Readers interested in examining his thought and his influence on twentieth century Protestant ethics might consult *American Protestant Ethics and the Legacy of H. Richard Niebuhr*, by William Werpehowski. Gerald McKenny has a penetrating essay on "Responsibility" in *The Oxford Handbook of Theological Ethics*. The classic philosophical treatment of consequentialist ethics is Henry Sidgwick's *Methods of Ethics*, though—be forewarned—the argument is long and complex. For an interesting and accessible deontological approach, written from a rather conservative Roman Catholic perspective, see *Beyond the New Morality*, by Germain Grisez and Russell Shaw. Alasdair MacIntyre's *After Virtue* was very influential in recapturing philosophical interest in virtue ethics, and a number of the early writings of Stanley Hauerwas do so in a theological vein.

Chapter Two

Volume 1 (on human nature) of Reinhold Niebuhr's *The Nature and Destiny of Man* continues to be well worth reading and considering for its discussion of human nature. And William F. May's *A Catalogue of Sins* offers an accessible and well-written treatment of pride and sloth. As a way of entry into Christian thought about original sin, one might read the discussion of Augustine and Pelagius in chapters 29, 30, and 31 of Peter Brown's marvelous biography, *Augustine of Hippo*. There are, of course, countless commentaries that might aid a reader in thinking through St. Paul's discussion of sin and grace in Romans. An accessible place to start would be Douglas J. Moo's *Encountering the Book of Romans: A Theological Survey*.

Chapter Three

Augustine's *Confessions* is an important and moving place to start when thinking about the work of divine grace in human beings. Translations abound. Henry Chadwick's (Oxford World Classics) and Rex Warner's (Signet Classics) are very readable. For Luther's programmatic treatise on "The Freedom of a Christian," the translation in volume 31 of the American Edition of *Luther's Works* (Fortress Press) is the place to turn. Readers who really want to enter deeply and at great length into an architectonic treatment of sin and grace could spend many hours working through volumes IV/1 and IV/2 of Karl Barth's *Church Dogmatics*.

Chapter Four

In his *Summa Theologiae* St. Thomas gives a detailed analysis of virtue and the virtues (a treatment that draws on Aristotle's

Nicomachean Ethics). For a marvelously lucid discussion that is essentially Thomistic see Josef Pieper's *The Four Cardinal Virtues*. And for a recent, clear discussion of the complexities of virtue in both Augustine and Aquinas, see Jean Porter, "Virtue," in *The Oxford Handbook of Theological Ethics*, ed. Gilbert Meilaender and William Werpehowski. A classic—if disputed—treatment of vocation is Max Weber's *The Protestant Ethic and the Spirit of Capitalism*. A more recent helpful (but long) discussion is Charles Taylor's *Sources of the Self*.

Chapter Five

Kierkegaard's short essay "Of the Difference Between a Genius and an Apostle," was published in Harper Torchbooks volume (1962), together with his essay "The Present Age." Three essays in *The Oxford Handbook of Theological Ethics* are relevant to the material in this chapter. They are "Ecclesiology and Ethics," by Bernd Wannenwetsch; "Tradition in the Church," by Philip Turner; and "Christians and the Church," by Paul J. Griffiths.

Chapter Six

On H. Richard Niebuhr one might (again) consult William Werpehowski, *American Protestant Ethics and the Legacy of H. Richard Niebuhr*. Also, D. M. Yeager, "H. Richard Niebuhr's *Christ and Culture*" in *The Oxford Handbook of Theological Ethics*; and Stassen, G. H., Yeager, D. M., and Yoder, J. H., *Authentic Transformation: A New Vision of Christ and Culture*. A standard translation of Augustine's *City of God* is the Penguin Books translation by Henry Bettenson. Luther's 1523 treatise, "Temporal

Authority: To What Extent It Should be Obeyed," is in volume 45 of the American edition of *Luther's Works.*

Chapter Seven

For a very clear discussion of the several different ways in which Christian love (agape) has been understood, Gene Outka's *Agape: An Ethical Analysis* will be very useful. Likewise, Josef Pieper's treatment in *Faith Hope Love* helpfully discusses the intricacies of saying to another, "It's good that you exist." There are many editions of *Jane Eyre*. An advantage of the Norton Critical (third) Edition is that, along with other critical discussion of the novel, it includes the essay by Jerome Beaty. For an exchange of views on *The Giving Tree*, see "*The Giving Tree*: A Symposium," in *First Things* (January 1995).

Chapter Eight

On the particular issue of preference in love, the text with which one must wrestle is surely Kierkegaard's *Works of Love*. Outka's *Agape* will again be helpful, as will Pieper's discussion of love, and chapter 1 of Gilbert Meilaender's *Friendship: A Study in Theological Ethics*. Augustine's discussion of love in Book One of *On Christian Doctrine* is readily available in D.W. Robertson, Jr.'s translation in the Library of Liberal Arts edition.

Chapter Nine

For Helmut Thielicke's very rich discussion of moral compromise, see chapter 25 (and then, in greater detail, successive chapters) in his *Theological Ethics, Volume I: Foundations*. Dietrich Bonhoeffer's little book, *Psalms: The Prayer Book of the Bible* is also available together with his *Life Together* in volume 5 of Bonhoeffer's Works (published by Fortress Press). For a discussion of some of the complications in Kierkegaard's *Fear and Trembling* see Gilbert Meilaender, "Freedom for the Command of God: Thinking with Johannes," in *The Freedom of a Christian* (Brazos Press).

Chapter Ten

For a detailed discussion of thought about the body in the first centuries of the Christian era, see Peter Brown's *The Body and Society: Men, Women, and Sexual Renunciation in Early Christianity*. Karl Barth's rich, even if flawed in certain respects, discussion of marriage (and more generally the relation of men and women) is in volume III/4 of his *Church Dogmatics*. A helpful treatment of marriage in the thought of many of the most important Christian thinkers (from the early Fathers to John Paul II) is Christopher Chenault Roberts' *Creation and Covenant: The Significance of Sexual Difference in the Moral Theology of Marriage*. In *The Oxford Handbook of Theological Ethics* see also Sondra Wheeler's essay, "Christians and Family."

Chapter Eleven

Readers wanting to explore further Lewis's thought on love should read his haunting "myth retold," *Till We Have Faces*. A different view from Lewis's, one that sets agape in sharp contrast with the natural loves can be found in Anders Nygren, *Agape and Eros*. More like Lewis is the view of Josef Pieper in *Faith, Hope, Love*.

INDEX